T0071944

BE READY FOR
ANYTHING

BE READY FOR ANYTHING

HOW TO SURVIVE TORNADOES, EARTHQUAKES, PANDEMICS, MASS SHOOTINGS, NUCLEAR DISASTERS, AND OTHER LIFE-THREATENING EVENTS

DAISY LUTHER

Racehorse Publishing

Copyright © 2019 by Daisy Luther

All rights reserved. No part of this book may be reproduced in any manner without the express written consent of the publisher, except in the case of brief excerpts in critical reviews or articles. All inquiries should be addressed to Skyhorse Publishing, 307 West 36th Street, 11th Floor, New York, NY 10018.

Racehorse Publishing books may be purchased in bulk at special discounts for sales promotion, corporate gifts, fund-raising, or educational purposes. Special editions can also be created to specifications. For details, contact the Special Sales Department, Skyhorse Publishing, 307 West 36th Street, 11th Floor, New York, NY 10018 or info@skyhorsepublishing.com.

Racehorse Publishing™ is a pending trademark of Skyhorse Publishing, Inc.®, a Delaware corporation.

Visit our website at www.skyhorsepublishing.com.

10 9 8 7 6 5 4 3 2 1

Library of Congress Cataloging-in-Publication Data is available on file.

Cover design by Daniel Brount
Cover photographs by iStockphoto

Print ISBN: 978-1-63158-392-6
Ebook ISBN: 978-1-63158-395-7

Printed in the United States of America

This book is dedicated to my father, who gave me the push I needed when he told me, "Writers write. They don't just talk about writing." I miss you and wish you could see this book.

TABLE OF CONTENTS

THE BASICS

If you are reading this book, you want to be prepared for whatever emergencies come your way. While prepping for a dozen different disasters may sound like a daunting task, there's good news. Preparing for a wide variety of disasters requires the same basic supplies as preparing for one or two. For each event, there will be some special steps, unique information, and precautions you need to take, along with a few additional supplies, but your essentials will be the same.

It would be incredibly boring if I reinvented the wheel in each chapter, so at the end of this book, there is a general guide to getting prepped. You'll also find checklists to help you stock up on food, water, and other important supplies. Those will be referenced in nearly every chapter so if you are new to prepping, you may want to read the last section first. (This may be the first time you'll ever be instructed to read the end of the book first!)

THE THREE-STEP SURVIVAL METHOD

Another common thread in surviving a variety of disasters is your mindset. Let me start out by telling you about three easy steps that can help you survive nearly anything. This is a lesson we'll talk about again and again throughout this book, so I think it's a great place to start. You can have enough food to ride out fifteen years of Armageddon. You can have a fully stocked retreat or bunker. You can have so much ammo stashed that your floorboards are groaning. You may have followed your favorite preparedness book's guidelines to the letter, and thus have all of the physical aspects of survival in place.

Despite all of this, you still may not be fully prepared because, surprisingly enough, none of these is an indication of "the prepper mindset." Those items are a great start, but to me, the pinnacle of preparedness is a way of thinking about pretty much everything you encounter. It's a unique way of looking at and accepting a situation, assessing the options and planning, and acting on that plan that defines the prepper mindset.

Think about any stressful or disastrous situation you've ever encountered. Once you accepted the fact that it happened, you were probably able to set a course of action. Once you had definitive steps to take, you probably felt much calmer. You took control of the things you could, and you executed your plan. Only by taking that first step—accepting that this mishap had indeed occurred—could you take the next one.

There are three steps to handling any crisis with aplomb. While the execution isn't always easy, making these steps second nature will greatly increase your chances of survival, no matter what kind of disaster you find yourself facing.

1. Accept

No matter what situation comes your way, the first step is to accept that whatever the event is, it really happened. This is tougher than it sounds, because our minds are programmed to protect us from emotional trauma. Cognitive dissonance means that when a reality is uncomfortable or doesn't jive with a person's beliefs, that person may opt to believe in something false just to assuage his desire for comfort. Psychologist Leon Festinger,[1] who identified the principle of cognitive dissonance, suggested that "a motivational state of inner tension is triggered by logically inconsistent ways of thinking."

If you're wondering exactly how powerful cognitive dissonance can be, check out journalist Amanda Ripley's book, *The Unthinkable: Who Survives When Disaster Strikes—and Why*. As a journalist, Ripley covered many disasters of immense scale: plane crashes, natural disasters, even 9/11. She became curious about the difference between those who survived, and those who did not, wondering if it was dumb luck or if there was some other quality that made survival more likely. She interviewed hundreds of survivors and got her answer. The ability to immediately accept what was occurring was the quality most of the survivors possessed. The story from her book that has always stood out the most in my mind is the one about the people in the World Trade Center on September 11, 2001. They described the last time they saw some of their coworkers. There were many people who simply could not accept the fact that a plane had crashed into the building and that they must immediately evacuate. They gathered their belongings, tidied their desks, finished reports. They didn't feel the same sense of urgency that those who survived did, because the situation was so horrible that they just couldn't accept it. Their inability to accept the scope of danger caused many of them to perish in a tragic incident that other people, who acted immediately, were able to survive. When disaster strikes, you can't spend five minutes thinking, *This can't actually be happening*. It *is* happening and accepting that propels you through the first step into the second one.

---

1   https://www.scribd.com/document/14068849/Cognitive-Consequences
    -of-Forced-Compliance-Leon-Festinger-James-Carlsmith-A-Psychology
    -Classic.

2. Plan

Once you've accepted that disaster has struck, you must devise a plan. It's a whole lot easier to come up with a plan if you've spent just a little bit of time doing that previously. This is where more mental preparedness skills come into play. To build your prepper mindset, I suggest having a prepper movie night or reading books about survival scenarios to help you develop the habit of watching the situations unfold and analyzing them. What would you do in such a situation? What are the potential pitfalls? What is likely to go wrong? Watching movies and reading books like this is sort of a dry run for actual events. Obviously, it's not the same as having an actual experience, but it's a good way to practice the skills of assessing a situation and making a plan.

You can also work on building your awareness. My friend Scott Kelley from Graywolf Survival[2] told me about "Kim's Game," a game based on *Kim*, a book by Rudyard Kipling, that teaches you to immediately observe your surroundings and commit these observations to memory. Groups of all ages, from the Boy Scouts to sniper schools to government spy agencies and surveillance teams, use this simple game to teach situational awareness and memory development. This is a fantastic game that you can play with your kids or teammates to help them be much better at noticing and remembering details. I have played a version of this with my kids for years, asking them questions like:

- What are three things you could use in this restaurant as a weapon?
- Can you find three ways out of this building?
- Can you close your eyes and tell me how many people are sitting at the counter? What do they look like?

---

2 http://graywolfsurvival.com/2173/using-kims-game-to-train-your-mind-for-survival/.

The habit of observing and absorbing information before a situation occurs will help in the creation of your plan. You don't have to spend the extra time taking in the specifics, because you've already done so automatically.

When you make your plan, don't stop at just one. The best-laid plans are at the mercy of a fluid situation, and disasters often come in bundles. If your Plan A doesn't work, you must immediately go back to square one and accept that it didn't work, then move on to Plan B.

3. Act

This is the step that will save your life. You've accepted the situation and made your plan. Now, it's time to act. This sounds easier than it is. Many people freeze in a disaster situation. The ability to break this paralysis is paramount to your survival.

"Freezing," referred to as "tonic immobility" in behavioral science, is a biological impulse. A study[3] by Norman B. Schmidt, J. Anthony Richey, Michael J. Zvolensky, and Jon K. Maner exploring the "freeze response" to stressors, describes the reaction: "Part of Barlow's (2002) description of an adaptive alarm model suggests that a freeze response may occur in some threatening situations. Specifically, freezing—or tonic immobility—may overwhelm other competing action tendencies. For example, when fleeing or aggressive responses are likely to be ineffective, a freeze response may take place. Similar to the flight/fight response, a freeze response is believed to have adaptive value. In the context of predatory attack, some animals will freeze or "play dead." This response, often referred to as tonic immobility (Gallup, 1977), includes motor and vocal inhibition with an abrupt initiation and cessation. Freezing in the context of an attack seems counterintuitive. However, tonic immobility may be the best option when the animal perceives little immediate chance of escaping or winning a fight (Arduino & Gould, 1984; Korte, Koolhaas, Wingfield, & McEwen,

---

3 http://www.ncbi.nlm.nih.gov/pmc/articles/PMC2489204/.

2005). For example, tonic immobility may be useful when additional attacks are provoked by movement or when immobility may increase the chance of escaping, such as when a predator believes its prey to be dead and releases it. Some of our data suggested that reports of freeze were more highly associated with certain cognitive symptoms of anxiety (e.g., confusion, unreality, detached, concentration, inner shakiness). This leads to some very interesting speculation regarding whether freeze responses are also manifested cognitively (i.e., the cognitive system, together with the behavioral system, being shut down). There has been some speculation that a form of cognitive paralysis occurs due to immense cognitive demands that occur in the context of life-threatening situations or stressors."

In the context of this particular study, the freeze response could be related to an overload of stimuli because of the demands of creating your plan. By having thought through various situations and getting into the habit of quickly developing plans, you can override your body's natural desire to "freeze" and you can take definitive, potentially lifesaving, action.

In an emergency, hesitation can kill you. The faster you can move through steps one and two, and then on to number three, the more likely you are to escape many disastrous situations. Please keep in mind that sometimes your action can seem like inaction. For example, a person who is aware they would have little chance of victory in a combative situation against a stronger, more experienced opponent might take the action of hiding and being very still. Sheltering in place in some situations is a better course of action than proceeding out into more danger. The key is to think clearly and assess each situation on its own merit. You don't have to be in the midst of a terrorist attack or on a crashing plane to apply the three steps above. Here are some examples of the three steps in action.

Job Loss: In this economy, the possibility of job loss is not that far-fetched. If the primary breadwinner in your home became suddenly unemployed, here's how the three-step survival method would apply:

Accept: The job is gone. The income source is gone. You can't go out to an expensive dinner like you'd planned, or take that pricey vacation, because as of now, you have no income; you must not act as though your income is the same as it was yesterday.

Plan: You go through your bank records. You check how much money is going out, how much you have, and figure out what expenses you can cut. You check your pantry and calculate how long the food will last.

Act: You take decisive action, immediately canceling cable, pushing back the family vacation indefinitely, sending out updated rewritten resumes, and dialing back the grocery bill. You sell some stuff just sitting in your basement and fill out the paperwork for unemployment insurance.

Car Accident: Sometimes the aftermath of an accident is more dangerous than the accident itself.

Accept: Your car is halfway down a ravine, held in place by a groaning tree that could give at any moment. Below you is a sheer drop off. You have to get your kids out of the car before it plunges further down, because no one could survive that.

Plan: You assess the kids and it seems everyone is conscious and relatively uninjured. The car, however, is not so great and could tumble the rest of the way down at any moment. The electronics of the car are working. You speak calmly to them and explain that they will be going out the back driver-side window one at a time. They are to immediately run to the left and get as far away from the vehicle as possible. You will be right behind them. The meeting point is the top of the hill by the big rock.

Act: You roll down the window, cut a jammed seat belt with the knife from the console, and wait for the kids to get out and clear of the vehicle. Then, you make your own escape.

Convenience Store Robbery: Occasionally, you're just in the wrong place at the wrong time.

Accept: As you're browsing through the cooler checking the price of a bottle of water, you hear a crash, then shouting up near the cash register. It's not a movie, a robbery is actually going down.

Plan: You listen and realize the criminal is armed. You are too, but you have your small children with you, so taking aggressive action is not an option. You decide that your best bet is to hide, but be ready to defend if necessary.

Act: You duck down and whisper to the kids to be quiet. You direct them to a hidey-hole, pull your weapon, and you get between them and anyone that might come down the aisle. Then, you wait.

Evacuation Order: This almost happened to us one year during forest fire season.

Accept: There is a giant fire drawing near. It is entirely possible that everything you own will go up in smoke. You have fifteen minutes to get out.

Plan: You gather what you need to get ready to leave. You grab the bug-out bags, the safe full of documents, the pet carriers, and the photo albums. You also get swim goggles for the whole family and respirator masks out of your kit.

Act: Pets, kids, and important items are loaded in the vehicle. You're already down the road in ten minutes, while other people are still trying to put together an overnight bag.

You'll see that this philosophy works in nearly every situation, and I'll mention it often throughout the book.

Now, let's learn about some disasters.

Chapter 1

HOW TO SURVIVE AN EARTHQUAKE

If you were caught up in the midst of a massive earthquake—the kind that takes down buildings and buckles roads—would you know what to do?

I'm not talking about a minor temblor that shakes a glass off the counter and sends it shattering on the floor.

I'm talking about the *Big One*. The one for which we are long overdue.

The United States has several active fault zones, and some of them are capable of producing extremely destructive quakes. While most people think of the West Coast as the most active (and for excellent reason), there are massive faults all over the US.

- The San Andreas Fault
- The Cascadia Fault
- The New Madrid Seismic Zone (This fault has fifteen nuclear power stations on it.[1])
- The Hayward Fault
- The Ramapo Fault
- The Puente Hills Fault

---

1   http://undergroundmedic.com/2016/09/is-the-new-madrid-fault-awakening-with-15-nuclear-power-plants-in-the-zone-lets-hope-not/.

All of these fault lines have ruptured before, and they will rupture again. In fact, more than half of the continental US could expect a major quake within the next fifty years.

That is just the continental United States! Alaska is at a very high risk of earthquakes, and Hawaii is in danger from tsunamis due to earthquakes in other parts of the Pacific.

National Geographic summarizes the risk:[2]

> *. . . while all U.S. states have some potential for earthquakes, 42 of the 50 states "have a reasonable chance of experiencing damaging ground shaking from an earthquake in 50 years," which is generally considered the typical lifetime of a building. Sixteen of those states have a "relatively high likelihood" of damaging shaking.*
>
> *With those odds, it's pretty likely that most of us will experience a significant earthquake in our lifetime.*

This chapter isn't about the long-term aftermath of an earthquake, during which you'd be unlikely to have power, safe water, or access to stores for supplies. It's about surviving the event itself.

HERE'S HOW TO SURVIVE AN EARTHQUAKE

So, what should you do when the ground starts shaking?

It depends on where you are. We'll go over three different scenarios. It's critical to note that sometimes people are just in the wrong place at the wrong time and that the situation will be very fluid. Be ready to adapt quickly if Plan A doesn't work.

The standard advice is to:

Drop: Get as low to the ground as possible.
Cover: Cover your head, get under something, and bend forward to protect your vital organs.

---

2   http://news.nationalgeographic.com/news/2014/07/140717-usgs
    -earthquake-maps-disaster-risk-science/.

Hold On: Hold on to your shelter with one hand and move along with it if it shifts.

Depending on the severity of the earthquake you may not get emergency announcements advising you of evacuation routes or refuge centers. The emergency services themselves may be unable to function, and communications may be down.

You could be on your own for a considerable length of time before rescuers get to you. It's vital to think clearly and logically, which is not always easy in an emergency. That's why it's important to think these things through ahead of time so that you've already made many of the necessary decisions well before the first sign of a tremor.

WHAT TO DO IF YOU'RE OUTSIDE DURING AN EARTHQUAKE

If you're outside, the biggest risk is being hit by something that has been structurally damaged by the quake.

- Move away from buildings to avoid getting hit by falling masonry.
- Avoid being near power lines.
- Move to the most open ground you can find (like a park or open space) which will decrease the danger from falling buildings or downed power lines.
- If you are within ten miles of the coast, head for higher ground immediately.
- If you are in your vehicle, stop in as open an area as possible. If you are on a ramp or a bridge, do not stop! *Get off it* immediately.
- Be alert for emergency announcements. If there are emergency announcements, follow the advice given.
- If there are not emergency announcements, start to consider your next move.

Hopefully, you and your family will have made a plan well ahead of time for a place to meet up safely.

WHAT TO DO IF YOU'RE AT THE BEACH DURING AN EARTHQUAKE

The biggest danger of experiencing an earthquake when you're at the beach is during the aftermath. A tsunami can travel as far as **ten** miles[3] inland, wiping out everything in its path. You will have no way of knowing where the epicenter of the quake was. The highest risk occurs when the epicenter is at sea. Here's a quick tsunami primer:[4]

> *Most tsunamis are caused by earthquakes. As a result, most tsunamis occur near or at fault lines. When a tsunami is generated, it is not only 1 wave. Instead it is a series of waves, known as a wave train. These waves travel together and can be up to 1 hour apart. Tsunami waves travel extremely fast with speeds of up to 500 miles per hour—the speed of a jet.*
>
> *They can be as wide as 60 miles and cross entire oceans without losing momentum. When a tsunami is traveling, it may be less than a foot in height. This causes it to be unnoticed by sailors who are at sea. As the tsunami approaches land, it hits shallow water and begins to slow down. The top of the wave, however, continues travelling, causing the sea to rise dramatically. Tsunamis are extremely destructive on land. The waves can surge up to 100 feet in height and completely devastate a coastal area.*

Tsunami waves travel at hundreds of miles per hour. You must act immediately because you will not be able to outrun it once it's close.

---

3   https://www.reference.com/science/far-inland-can-tsunami-a0fed181ad259ced.

4   https://www.reference.com/science/tsunami-happen-7cb4551242581d56?qo=contentSimilarQuestions.

- Move inland and to higher ground as far and as fast as you can.
- If there are tsunami evacuation routes marked, follow them.
- If you see the water recede dramatically, move out of the way—you have only moments before the tsunami hits.

After the initial wave, it is *extremely likely* that more will follow. These waves can be up to an hour apart. Do not return to lower ground until officials have given the all-clear.

WHAT TO DO IF YOU'RE INDOORS DURING AN EARTHQUAKE

If you are inside when a quake occurs, your priority is to protect yourself until you can escape the building and get to a place in the open, like I talked about earlier. Staying in a building can put you at great risk in the event that the building collapses.

These tips will help you to remain safe if you are indoors when an earthquake hits:

- Move away from the windows immediately. They can shatter.
- Move away from exterior walls. In a *very* severe quake, the sides of buildings can give way.
- Move away from any shelves, cabinets, or other loose items that could fall on you.
- Take shelter in or under the sturdiest thing you can find. Stairwells can be a good option if you are close to one. Otherwise, duck under a sturdy desk or table (not the cruddy fiberboard kind, obviously).
- Cover your head as added protection. Grab whatever you can find. Large books, a chair, or even a briefcase held over your head can help protect you from falling debris.

If you are at home when disaster strikes, the same rules apply. Don't let familiarity with your surroundings lull you into a false sense of security.

WHAT TO DO IMMEDIATELY AFTER AN EARTHQUAKE

Remember that aftershocks can often be as powerful (or even more so) as the initial event. There is no reliable way to predict how soon those shocks will arrive.

As soon as the shaking stops, you need to assess your situation as quickly and calmly as possible.

- **From your sheltered position, survey the area.** Look for hanging light fixtures and exposed wires. These could be live and cause electrocution.
- **When you emerge from your temporary shelter, scan the area ahead of you.** Look for open wiring, broken pipes, holes in floors, and other hazards.
- ***Do not* use elevators to evacuate from a higher floor**, even though it may seem quicker. Not only could the power go off, trapping you, but there could also be damage of which you are unaware. Don't risk plummeting to your death because you didn't want to take the stairs.
- **Move slowly and carefully toward the nearest exit.** Then pause and assess the outlying areas. Are the stairs still intact enough to use? If not, is there another flight of stairs that you can get to from your current position?
- **Be prepared to move laterally to other areas to find the safest escape route.** If you are trapped on upper floors, look for "staff only" doors which may lead to service stairways and exit doors that may be less damaged.
- **When you reach the ground floor (or if you're already on it), don't just rush out of the building as fast as you can.** Pause and see if anything is falling in front of you. The risk from falling debris immediately after an earthquake is extremely high.
- **If your exit to the outside is blocked, be *very cautious* in moving debris to escape.** Try to assess what that wood, concrete, or metal is holding up before you move it.

The slightest shift has the potential to cause a collapse. Before moving the debris, see if other exits might be less risky.

HOW TO SAFELY EVACUATE AFTER AN EARTHQUAKE

If you need to leave the immediate area, here are a few things to keep in mind to travel safely.

- Avoid underpasses, overpasses, and bridges. They may be structurally unsound.
- Stay as far away from buildings as you can.
- Be on the lookout for potential hazards such as downed power lines or leaning trees.
- Crevasses caused by earthquakes can be very deep. Injury or even death could occur if you step or drive into one.
- Stay as far away as you can from dikes and levees, which may have sustained structural damage. If they rupture, the force of the water will be immense.

If you are near major fault lines, it's essential to know not only what to do during and just after an earthquake, but to be prepared to survive for a while without assistance. You'll need food, water, climate control, and other supplies to last up to a month or longer.

To find out more about surviving the aftermath of an earthquake, refer to:

Appendix 2: Emergency Food Basics (pg. 151)
Appendix 3: Emergency Water Basics (pg. 157)
Appendix 4: Power Outage Survival Basics (pg. 167)
Appendix 6: Emergency Sanitation Basics (pg. 185)
Appendix 8: First Aid Kit Basics (pg. 197).

Chapter 2

HOW TO SURVIVE
A TORNADO

Anyone who lives in certain parts of the country knows the signs of an approaching tornado. The wind is whipping things around, and the sky turns an indescribably dark yellow-green color. Sometimes there's hail and heavy rain that suddenly stops. The wind changes. And there's nearly always a loud, persistent roar that becomes more deafening the closer the tornado gets. When you see signs like that, you know it's time to take shelter immediately. These days, we have more advanced warning systems that dispatch warnings to cell phones in a local area; TV stations interrupt programming; and warning sirens begin blaring.

Tornadoes can appear quickly and without any warning, so your goal should be to have a shelter with supplies already set up well before the wind starts to blow. Once you can see the twister, you won't have time for anything but getting to the shelter.

WHERE TO SHELTER IF YOU'RE AT HOME

First things first. Mobile homes are *absolutely not safe* in a tornado, no matter how well they are secured. If you live in a mobile home, you should have a secondary underground shelter or seek shelter in a nearby building. Creating a tornado shelter is something everyone in tornado-prone areas should do. Because we all have different settings, here are the best places to shelter at home.

1. **The best bet is a storm cellar that has been dug outside the home.** These are superior because there is less risk of being trapped in there by the debris of the house above it. It should be in a location that allows quick access but isn't so close that the house can collapse upon it. For this reason, you'll see that many storm shelters have doors set at an angle. Keep supplies like food, water, sanitary products, and first aid kits in the shelter in case you are stuck in there for a while.

2. **The next safest place is the basement of your home.** Find a spot in the basement that isn't directly under something heavy on the main floor, like a piano or a refrigerator. Make sure you are as far away from any windows as possible. In that area, place some kind of sturdy protection like a heavy table, desk, or workbench. Keep the area underneath it clear so that you and your family can take shelter in it immediately. Keep mattresses or sleeping bags nearby to pull over everyone to protect them from flying glass and debris. For extra protection, keep helmets (bicycle, football, etc.) in the area.

3. **If you don't have a basement, find the most protected spot.** Go to the lowest floor possible and find a place that is close to the center, without any exterior doors or windows. Get in a bathtub and pull a mattress or something sturdy over your family. Alternatively, seek shelter in a windowless hallway, under the stairs, or in a closet. Always try to pull something over yourself and your family like a twin-sized mattress or blankets to help protect you from debris or flying glass.

WHAT TO DO IF YOU'RE NOT AT HOME

I'll never forget when a tornado hit our school when I was in ninth grade. The noise was deafening and when it hit, I could no longer hear the kids who were crying and screaming. We crouched in the hallway and stuck our heads in our lockers as directed. Fortunately, no one was seriously injured but it left an indelible impression of the power of Mother Nature.

If you are not at home, but you are indoors, go to the lowest level of the building you can get to. Stay in the center of the building if possible—stairwells are a good option. Stay as far away from windows, doors, and potentially deadly flying glass as possible. Stay out of large, open spaces like gyms and auditoriums. *Do not* take an elevator to try to get to a lower floor faster.

WHAT TO DO IF YOU'RE DRIVING

If you happen to be in your car or truck when there is a tornado headed your way, you're stuck with the slightly-less-deadly option over the definitely-deadly option. If it's far enough away, you may be able to get out of the path of the storm by turning at right angles, but keep in mind that tornadoes are prone to changing directions quickly.

If you can find a low place like a ditch to get to, exit your vehicle and lay face down at the lowest possible point. Cover your head with your hands and, if possible, bring a blanket or coat from the car to put over yourself.

If there are no low points, pull off the road, turn off your car, and remain seat belted. Cover yourself with a coat or blanket and tuck your head below the level of the windows. *Do not park under a bridge or overpass.*

WHAT TO DO IF YOU'RE OUTSIDE

If you are outdoors, try to get to a sturdy building. If you are not able to get to a sturdy building, find the lowest point possible (like a ditch) to lie down, and cover your head with your arms. If there is no low point where you can seek shelter, lie down flat on your stomach and cover your head with your arms. Stay as far away as you can from trees, cars, and other large objects that could fall or be blown onto you.

WHAT TO DO AFTER A TORNADO

Just like an earthquake, the aftermath of a tornado can be just as deadly as the twister itself. Keep family members close together and warn children not to touch *anything*. If anyone is injured, give them first aid.

Watch out for:

- Downed power lines
- Puddles with wires in them
- Broken glass
- Nails
- Sharp debris
- Raw sewage

Do not go into any damaged buildings because they could collapse. Do not use matches or cigarette lighters. If a natural gas pipe or fuel tank is leaking, they could explode with the introduction of a flame.

If you have vulnerable neighbors, check to see if they need help.

Before you touch anything or try to set it to rights, take pictures of everything with your phone. You'll need this for insurance purposes.

Check your phone, radio, or television for news. Emergency crews will most likely be out soon to render assistance and provide further information. If not, you need to check for hazards.

- **Electrical Issues:** Be on the alert for sparks, frayed wires, or burning smells. If you detect any of those, turn off the main breaker to the house only if you can get to it without stepping in water. Call an electrician.
- **Gas Leaks:** If you smell gas or hear a hissing noise, open the window and get everyone out of the building immediately. Turn off the gas at the exterior valve and contact the gas company.

- **Chemical Spills:** If substances like medicines, bleaches, gasoline, or other flammable liquids have spilled, clean them up as quickly as possible.

If you live in a tornado-prone area, make sure your children know what to do in the event of a tornado. It could save their lives if they are home alone or at school when one strikes.

Resources:
Appendix 4: Power Outage Survival Basics (pg. 167)
Appendix 8: First Aid Kit Basics (pg. 197)

Chapter 3
HOW TO SURVIVE
A HURRICANE

While it's often best to evacuate when a hurricane is on its way, there are reasons that some people are unable to get out in time. While it's easy to say, "Oh, they should have left earlier," and run through the gamut of blame, the fact remains that there are all sorts of reasons that leaving didn't work out.

Gas stations could have run dry, which means that people can't drive their cars to leave. Roads may be at a standstill as people all try to leave at once in a mass exodus. Amtrak tickets could be sold out. Plane tickets are outrageously expensive, in some cases more than three thousand dollars *apiece* when you're booking last minute.

I can't urge you strongly enough, evacuate if you can. Learn about Evacuation Basics in Appendix 5 (pg. 173). Hurricanes can quickly become life-threatening emergencies. But if you don't have that option, this chapter discusses what to do to survive when the hurricane strikes.

Here's an explanation of hurricane categories.
Hurricane categories are based on the Saffir–Simpson hurricane wind scale.

- Category 1: 74–95 mph
- Category 2: 96–110 mph
- Category 3: 111–129 mph

- Category 4: 130–156 mph
- Category 5: any hurricane with winds of 157 mph or greater

Never be deluded by saying that a hurricane is "only" a Category 3. So was Hurricane Katrina, and that disaster caused record-setting, catastrophic damage to New Orleans, Louisiana.

WHAT TO DO IF YOU CAN'T EVACUATE

If you've waited too long to evacuate, it may also be difficult to find the supplies that you need.

Remember, there comes a point at which it's too late to order supplies online. There is practically no chance that the items will reach you in time, so you're going to need to choose from whatever happens to be left at the local stores. (And trust me, you'll have competition for those items.) You may not be able to buy standard hurricane supplies at the store at this point, either, so you'll have to make do with what you have or can still acquire.

Let me be absolutely clear, lest someone accuse me of recommending that people remain in their homes: **remaining at home is *not* a wise course of action when a hurricane is headed your way.** If you need help evacuating, contact your local authorities who may be able to aid you in getting to a safe shelter before the storm hits. Do not wait until the storm hits to ask for help. Be proactive and do so ahead of time.

If you have *absolutely no other option*, below, you will find the best advice I can offer.

Water

Water is sold out across the state, but your taps are running just fine, right?

Fill every container you can get your hands on with tap water so that you have something to drink. If you can't buy bottled water, it's likely that you can still buy containers that will hold water. Get Mason jars, pitchers, canisters, whatever you can find to hold water, then fill *all* of them immediately. Use empty soda bottles or water jugs, too.

Fill one-gallon re-sealable bags with water and freeze them, allowing room for expansion. Not only will this provide drinking water, but the ice will help keep your food safe for longer.

When the storm is about to hit, fill sinks and bathtubs with water. This can be used for sanitation. (See Appendix 3: Emergency Water Basics on page 157 for more information.)

Medications

Fill prescriptions for any essential medications immediately. Plan for at least two weeks of medication to be on hand in case pharmacies are closed after the storm. Make sure you have basic OTC remedies like pain relievers, antidiarrheals, antihistamines, cold medicine, and nausea medication.

Food

If there's anything available, buy food that doesn't require any cooking. At this point, you can't afford to be picky. Get enough for at least a week, preferably two. (See Appendix 2: Emergency Food Basics on page 151 for more information.)

Cash

Keep some cash on hand, preferably in small bills. If there is a regional power outage, you won't be able to use a debit or credit card during the aftermath. I suggest keeping several hundred dollars in ones, fives, and tens, if you can.

Shelter

Generally, there are shelters set up when a hurricane is on its way. Be sure to get there early—if you wait until the storm hits, you've waited too long—particularly if you are in a manufactured or mobile home as there is practically zero chance it will be able to withstand winds of 150 mph or greater.

Prepare your home by doing the following:

- **Secure anything outside that could become a projectile** (barbecues, bicycles, outdoor furniture, etc.). If you can't secure the items, bring them inside.
- **Clear your rain gutters and downspouts.** This will help reduce the risk of flooding and leaking roofs in some cases.
- **Trim trees.** If you have branches hanging over your home, remove them if you can. If you can't, do not use the room beneath the branches for shelter during the storm.
- **Turn off propane** and outdoor utilities. If recommended by officials, turn off the utilities to the house. If the power goes out, turn off your breakers to avoid potential surges.
- **Unplug appliances except for the refrigerator and freezer.** Set those at the coldest setting to keep your food safe for as long as possible in the event of a power outage.
- **Board up your windows** to reduce the risk of injury from flying glass. Keep curtains closed for added protection. Do *not* tape them—this will not prevent them from imploding and will simply send larger shards of glass your way.
- **Secure exterior doors.** While it may not be sufficient, you can use a bar or place a large piece of furniture in front of them.
- **Close all interior doors.**
- **Find the innermost, sturdiest part of your home** in which to take shelter during the worst part of the storm. Stay away from windows and skylights. A downstairs closet, hallway, or bathroom may be the best option. If you have a basement, this could provide the most safety. Shelter under a sturdy piece of furniture if you have no such area.
- **In a high-rise building, the third to tenth floors are considered to be the safest.** Above and below those floors, people should evacuate or take shelter between those floors.

- **Watch for storm surges.** If you're near the coast, storm surges of ten to twenty feet are often expected. Not only can these cause tremendous structural damage, but if you are caught in one, you could drown or suffer serious injuries by being slammed around by the water.
- **Don't be fooled by the eye of the storm.** There is a lull during the eye of the storm that can deceive people into believing the worst is over. Unfortunately, high winds are likely to pick back up again shortly, so don't be caught off guard. This lull can last anywhere from five to forty-five minutes.

THE AFTERMATH

Once you've survived the hurricane, you must take care to survive the aftermath. As we saw during Hurricane Harvey in 2017, a disaster of this level is the gift that keeps on giving. They had flooding, looters, and a chemical plant that exploded, just to name a few subsequent disasters.

After a hurricane, you must watch for:

- Flooding
- Health risks related to flooding
- Downed power lines
- Looters
- Industrial dangers like explosions, nuclear emergencies, and chemical spills

Just to name a few!

Don't let your guard down once the hurricane has passed, because for many, that means the long-term disaster has just begun.

References for surviving the aftermath of the hurricane:

Chapter 4

HOW TO SURVIVE
A WINTER STORM

If you live in certain climates, blizzards are going to occur every winter. Typically, at least one storm hits that will cause you to be snowed in or even lose power. Few can deny the common sense behind preparing for something that is definitely going to happen, yet every year an impending winter storm sends people rushing out to the store at the last minute, prepping for a blizzard that is due to hit in mere hours.

But you can avoid all that. You don't have to be a bunker-dwelling, MRE-chomping, camo-clad prepper to see the logic behind keeping some extra food and other supplies on hand for something that happens every single year. This year, avoid the last-minute panic and the discomfort of being unprepared. Put together at least a minimum kit for riding out the storm. (Camo is optional.)

WATER

Everyone knows that clean drinking water is something you can't live without. In the event of a blizzard and power outage, the water may not run from the taps. The pipes could freeze, or in the event of grid failure, an electrically driven pump will not work.

"I'll just eat snow." No, this is a horrible idea! First of all, snow is mostly air, and you'd have to eat twenty quarts of it to equal two quarts of water. Secondly, if you eat that much snow you will lower your core temperature and put yourself at risk for hypothermia. If you already don't have water, you have enough problems. You don't need hypothermia on top of that.

For a small amount of money, you can have one five-gallon jug of water sitting in your closet, instead of melting snow, crouched beside a fire in the backyard, watching the pot. You aren't in the wilderness fending off bears. This really is not a good plan. First of all, the snow picks up all sorts of pollution as it falls through the atmosphere. The impurities can potentially make you sick. In a poorly thought-out situation in which snow is your only hope for survival, boil it for ten minutes before drinking it. Then, when the crisis is over, please store some water so you never have to do this again.

Each family should store a two-week supply of water. The rule of thumb for drinking water is one gallon per day, per person. Don't forget to stock water for your pets, also. The amount of water your pets will need varies by their size but is usually half a gallon to a gallon each.

See Appendix 3 (pg. 157) for more detailed information on creating an emergency water supply.

FOOD

Enough with the milk and bread already. Do you even consume milk and bread on a regular basis? This is really not the food you want to propel you through shoveling a driveway seventeen times until the plow goes past, at which point you will have to shovel it again.

There are two schools of thought regarding food during a power outage. One: you need a cooking method that does not require the grid to be functional. Two: you can store food that doesn't require cooking. This is a good idea if you don't have an emergency stove or wood heat.

If you opt for a secondary cooking method, be sure that you have enough fuel for two weeks. Store foods that do not require long cooking times. For example, dried beans would use a great deal of fuel, but canned beans could be warmed up, or even eaten cold.

See Appendix 2 (pg. 151) for more information about building an emergency food supply.

HEAT

Freezing to death in your own home would be a terrible way to go, wouldn't it? It's pretty anticlimactic. There's no grand story of adventure. Before the storm even happens, there are some ways that you can practice staying warm with less heat than normal.

Not only do we need to be concerned about a power outage due to weather, but we also need to realize that utility bills could become extraordinarily high due to rising prices and an increased need for heat as temperatures plummet. When we lived in our drafty cabin up north, we had to take extra steps to keep warm.

These strategies will help you use less heat during normal times and manage with secondary or no heat during emergencies:

- **Keep your wrists and ankles covered.** Wear shirts with sleeves long enough to keep your wrists covered and long socks that keep your ankles covered. You lose a great deal of heat from those two areas.
- **Get some long johns.** Wearing long underwear beneath your jeans or pj's will work like insulation to keep your body heat in. I like the silky kind for indoor use, rather than the chunkier waffle-knit outdoor type.
- **Wear slippers.** You want to select house shoes with a solid bottom rather than the slipper sock type. This forms a barrier between your feet and the cold floor. We keep a basket of inexpensive slippers in varying sizes by the door for visitors because it makes such a big difference. Going around in your stockinged feet on a cold floor is a certain way to be chilled right through.
- **Get up and get moving.** It goes without saying that physical activity will increase your body temperature. If you're cold, get up and clean something, dance with your kids, play tug-of-war with the dog, or do a chore.

- **Pile on the blankets.** If you're going to be sitting down, have some blankets available for layering. Our reading area has some plush blankets which we top with fluffy comforters for a cozy place to relax.
- **Use a hot water bottle.** If you're just sitting around try placing a hot water bottle (carefully wrapped to avoid burns) under the blankets with you.
- **Use rice bags.** If you don't have the cute, ready-made rice bags, you can simply place dry rice in a clean sock. Heat this in the microwave, if you use one, for about a minute, or place in a 100°F oven, watching carefully, for about 10 minutes. I keep some rice bags in a large ceramic crock beside the wood stove, so they are constantly warm. You can put your feet on them or tuck them under the blankets on your lap. (The insert from a defunct crockpot will work for this as well.)
- **Insulate using items you have.** A friend recommended lining the interior walls with bookcases or hanging decorative quilts and blankets on the walls to add an extra layer of insulation. It definitely makes a difference because it keeps heat in and cold air out. If you look at pictures of old castles you will see lovely tapestry wall-hangings, this was to help insulate the stone walls, which absorbed the cold and released it into the space.
- **Layer your windows.** Our cabin had large lovely picture windows for enjoying the view. However, they were single pane, and it's hard to enjoy the view if your teeth are chattering, so we took the rather drastic step of basically closing off all the windows but one in each room for the winter. We do this by first using shrink film insulator on every window. Then, we insulate further by placing draft blockers at the bottom of the windowsill (I just use rolled-up polar fleece— I'm not much of a sewer). This gets topped by a heavy blanket, taking care to overlap the wall and window edges with it. Over that, we hang thermal curtains that remain closed.

- **Get a rug.** If you have hardwood, tile, or laminate flooring, an area rug is a must. Like the blankets on the walls, this is another layer of insulation between you and the great out- doors. We had no basement in our cabin, so our floor was very chilly. A rug in the living room protects our feet from the chill.
- **Wear a scarf.** No, not like a big heavy wool scarf that you'd wear outdoors, just a small, lightweight one that won't get in your way and annoy you. This serves two purposes. First, it covers a bit more exposed skin. Second, it keeps body heat from escaping out the neck of your shirt.
- **Burn candles.** Especially in a smaller space, a burning candle can raise the temperature a couple of degrees.
- **Wear fingerless gloves.** Gloves like these allow you to function by keeping the tips of your fingers uncovered, while still keeping chilly hands bundled up.
- **Drink hot beverages.** There's a reason Grandma always gave you a mug of cocoa after you finished building that snowman. Warm up from the inside out with a cup of coffee, tea, cider, or hot chocolate. Bonus: holding the mug makes your hands toasty warm.
- **Cuddle.** Share your body heat under the blankets when you're watching movies or reading a book.

That will work to help you stay warm using less heat than normal, but what if there's no heat at all? The best option is secondary heat methods.

Here are some options for heat that don't come from a thermo- stat on the wall.

- **Wood Heat:** Everyone's favorite off-grid heating method is a fireplace or wood stove. The fuel is renewable, and you have the added bonus of an off-grid cooking method. Unfortunately, if your home doesn't already have one, it can be a pretty expensive thing to install. If you rent, it's probably not going to be an option at all to add wood heat to someone else's property. If you have wood heat, make sure you have a good supply of seasoned firewood that is well-protected from the elements.

- **Propane Heaters:** There are several propane heaters on the market that do not require electricity. I own a Little Buddy heater. These small portable heaters are considered safe for indoor use in forty-nine states. They attach to a small propane canister and use two ounces of fuel per hour to make one hundred square feet extremely warm and toasty. A battery-operated carbon monoxide alarm provides an extra measure of safety when using these heaters indoors. If you have a bigger area to heat, the larger unit will warm up to two hundred square feet. Be sure to stock up on propane if this is your backup heat method.

- **Kerosene/Oil Heaters:** Kerosene heaters burn a wick for heat, fueled by the addition of heating oil. These heaters really throw out the warmth. A brand-new convection kerosene heater can heat up to one thousand square feet efficiently. When we lived in the city, I was lucky enough to have an antique Perfection[1] oil heater, a charming addition to our decor that was called into service during grid-down situations.

- **Natural Gas Fireplaces:** Some gas-fueled fireplaces will work when the electrical power goes out—they just won't blow out heat via the fan.

- **Pellet Stove:** Most pellet stoves require electricity to run, but there are a few of these high-efficiency beauties that will work without being plugged in, the most famous of which is Wiseway.

---

1   http://www.milesstair.com/Perfection_History.htm.

What if you don't have a secondary heating method?

Sometimes things happen before we get our preps in order. If you don't have a secondary heating method, you can still stay relatively warm for at least a couple of days if you are strategic. Even if you do have a secondary heat source, in many cases it's important to conserve your fuel as much as possible.

If the cold is relentless and the outage lasts longer than a day or two, you may need to seek other shelter. Watch your temperatures. If the daytime temperature in the house dips below 40°F, the nighttime temperature will be even colder, and it won't be safe to stay there, especially if you have children or family members who are more susceptible to illness.

During the first twenty-four hours after a power outage, you can stay fairly warm using the following tips.

- **Heat only one room.** One year, our furnace went out the day before Christmas. We huddled into a small room with just one window. We closed the door to the bedroom and used a folded quilt at the bottom to better insulate the room. If you don't have a door to the room you've opted to take shelter in, you can hang heavy quilts or blankets in the doorways to block it off from the rest of the house.
- **Block drafts.** Roll up towels or place sandbags at the bottoms of doors and windows to help reduce drafts from the outside and keep the warmth inside.
- **Cover your windows and doors:** You can use a plastic shower curtain and duct tape, topped by a heavy quilt to keep the wind from whistling through your windows. Take down the quilt if it's sunny outside for some solar gain, then cover it back up as darkness falls. If you have reason to be concerned about OPSEC, use heavy black garbage bags to cover the windows to keep light from escaping.
- **Light candles.** Even the small flames from candles can add warmth to a small area. Be sure to use them safely by

keeping them out of the reach of children and housing them in holders that won't tip over easily.

- **Use kerosene lamps.** Those charming old-fashioned lamps can also add warmth to the room.
- **Use sleeping bags.** Cocooning in a sleeping bag conserves body heat better than simply getting under the covers.
- **Have a campout.** This works especially well when you have children because it adds an element of fun to an otherwise stressful situation. Pitch a tent in your closed off room, get inside with a flashlight, and tell stories. When you combine your body heat in a tiny space like that, you'll stay much warmer.
- **Get cooking.** If you have a propane or gas stove in the kitchen, your cooking method may not require electricity. Bake a cake, roast a turkey, or simmer a soup. You can use it to warm the room while making a hot, delicious feast.
- **Heat some rocks.** Do you have a place outdoors for a campfire? If so, put some large rocks around the edges of it. They retain heat for hours. When it's bedtime, carefully place the rocks into a cast-iron Dutch oven and bring this into the room you're going to be sleeping in. Be sure to protect your floor or surface from the heat of the Dutch oven. The stones will passively emit heat for several hours without the potential of a fire or carbon monoxide poisoning during the night.

Just remember, after about forty-eight hours, these tips will not be enough in very cold weather. You will require backup heat at this point. If you are lucky enough to have a source of heat like a fireplace or wood stove, you'll be just fine as long as you have a supply of dry, seasoned firewood.

SANITATION

A common cause of illness or even death during a grid-down scenario is the lack of sanitation. We've discussed the importance of clean drinking water, but you won't want to use your drinking water to keep things clean or to flush the toilet. If the pipes are frozen or you have no running water for other reasons during a winter storm, you'll need to consider sanitation needs.

- For cleaning, reduce your need to wash things with disposable items.
- Keep bleach wipes and hand sanitizer for emergencies.
- Set up hand-washing stations in the kitchen with a pitcher, bowl, and soap.
- Figure out your bathroom sanitation plan.

See Appendix 6 (pg. 185) for more information about sanitation.

LIGHT

Lighting is absolutely vital, especially if there are children in the house. Nothing is more frightening than being completely in the dark during a stressful situation. Fortunately, it's one of the easiest things to plan for, as well as one of the least expensive. Candles and kerosene lamps are especially good during a winter power outage because they add a small amount of heat. However, if you have small children or pets, you may be concerned about the risk of fire.

See Appendix 4 (pg. 167) for more information on emergency lighting.

SPECIAL NEED ITEMS

These items will be unique to every family. Consider the things that are needed on a daily basis in your household. It might be prescription medications, diapers, or special foods. If you have pets, you'll need supplies for them too. The best way to figure out what you'll need is to jot things down as you use them over the course of a week or so.

More information in Appendix 4 (pg. 167).

OUTDOOR TOOLS AND SUPPLIES

In the event of a winter storm, you'll need some special supplies in order to keep walkways and steps clear and less hazardous:

- Snow shovel
- Snowblower
- Salt

Exercise that you're unaccustomed to is one of the most frequent causes of death in the aftermath of a snow storm. Many people drop dead of a heart attack shoveling their driveways. If you aren't in shape, be sure that you use good sense when performing strenuous tasks. Take frequent breaks, stop when you're out of breath, and do only a little bit at a time. Be sure to dress appropriately for the weather.

What if you're stranded due to icy roads?

What if you're not at home when a winter storm strikes? Here are some real-life examples of why you need to have an emergency kit in your vehicle. (See Appendix 7 on page 193 to learn more about a vehicle emergency kit.)

During one scenario, a freak snowstorm struck the Atlanta, Georgia area.[2] Because weather like this is such a rarity, the area was completely unprepared, officials didn't have the experience or equipment needed to deal with it, and traffic gridlocked almost immediately. Hundreds of people were stranded as the freeway turned into a scene reminiscent of *The Walking Dead*, with bumper-to-bumper vehicles at a standstill. Those without food and water in their vehicles went hungry, and many people ran out of gas as they tried to keep warm. No matter how comfortable you are with winter driving, in a situation like this, you are at the mercy of others who may not be so experienced.

---

2   https://www.theorganicprepper.com/stranded-freak-snowstorm-in-the -south-results-in-epic-overnight-gridlock.

The next situation had a lot more potential for a tragic ending, had it not been for the survival skills of a father of four small children. A family of six had taken off for a day of snowy adventure, when their Jeep flipped over in a remote part of the Seven Troughs mountain range in northwestern Nevada.[3] James Glanton, a miner and experienced hunter, kept his family alive and unscathed for two days in the frigid wilderness using only the items from his vehicle and the environment. Due to his survival skills and the items he kept on hand, none of the family members suffered so much as frostbite while awaiting rescue.

Regardless of why you're stranded somewhere outside your cozy home, you should have enough supplies in your vehicle to fend off frostbite (or even death) due to frigid conditions.

Even if you aren't a full-fledged prepper, it only makes sense to get ready for a storm.

Winters in America have been setting records for bone-numbing, snot-freezing cold for the last couple of years, so it's safe to say that this winter will be no different. While some folks aren't quite ready to plunge wholeheartedly into prepping, it's hard to deny the common-sense factor of preparing for a likely scenario. You should have, at minimum, a two-week supply of food and other necessities. Before the power goes out, develop a plan to keep your family warm, even while the mercury outside reaches near-Arctic depths.

---

3   https://www.theorganicprepper.com/real-life-survival-could-you-stay
-alive-in-the-frigid-wilderness-with-only-the-supplies-in-your-vehicle.

Chapter 5

HOW TO SURVIVE A SUMMER POWER OUTAGE

Sometimes people think that a summer power outage is easier to deal with than a winter one. After all, in the summer, you don't have to worry about freezing to death, which is a very real threat during a long-lasting winter outage.

However, a summer power outage carries its own set of problems. Foremost are heat-related illnesses and the higher potential of spoilage for your food. Even if you aren't convinced that hardcore preparedness is for you, it would still be difficult to argue against the possibility of a disaster that takes out the power for a couple of weeks. Basic emergency preparedness is important for everyone, not just us "crazy preppers."

Just ask the people who lived through the derecho of 2012. Severe, fast-moving thunderstorms (called derechos) swept through Indiana, Ohio, Virginia, West Virginia, Pennsylvania, Maryland, New Jersey, and Washington DC, causing millions of people to lose power, an estimated 4 million for an entire week. As if a week-long power outage wasn't miserable enough, that part of the country was in the midst of a record-setting heat wave at the time.

Also keep in mind that summer stresses our fragile power grid to the max, as everyone increases their usage of electricity to try and keep cool with air conditioners and fans. This ups the chances of an outage even when there's not a cloud in the sky. Back in 2003, a software bug caused an extremely widespread power outage in the middle of August. It was a very hot day, and increased energy demand overloaded the system. Because of the issue with the software, engineers were not alerted of this, and what should have been a small local outage turned into an event that took out power for over 10 million Canadians and 45 million Americans. I remember this one clearly because the little sub shop beside my workplace gave away all the perishable food that they had out at the time before it spoiled, and I took home fresh sandwiches for my girls' dinner that night. We sweated uncomfortably through the next two days until the power was restored.

DEHYDRATION AND HEAT-RELATED ILLNESSES

One of the most serious concerns that sets apart a summer power outage from that of other times of the year is the heat. When you don't have so much as a fan to move the air around, heat-related illnesses and dehydration are strong possibilities.

Dehydration is the state that occurs when you use or lose more fluid than you take in, and your body doesn't have enough water and other fluids to carry out its normal functions. Your electrolytes are out of balance, which can lead to increasingly serious problems.

Symptoms of electrolyte imbalances include headaches, dizziness, fatigue, nausea (with or without vomiting), constipation, dry mouth, dry skin, muscle weakness, stiff or aching joints, confusion, delirium, rapid heart rate, twitching, blood pressure changes, seizures, and convulsions.

Dehydration can lead to very serious side effects, including death. Following are the most common dehydration-related ailments:

Heat cramps: Heat cramps are painful, brief muscle cramps. Muscles may spasm or jerk involuntarily. Heat cramps can occur during exercise or work in a hot environment or begin a few hours following such activities.

Heat exhaustion: Often accompanied by dehydration, heat exhaustion is a heat-related illness that can occur after you've been exposed to high temperatures.

There are two types of heat exhaustion:

- **Water depletion:** Signs include excessive thirst, weakness, headache, and loss of consciousness.
- **Salt depletion:** Signs include nausea and vomiting, muscle cramps, and dizziness.

Heat stroke: Heat stroke is the most serious form of heat injury and is considered a medical emergency. Heat stroke results from prolonged exposure to high temperatures—usually in combination with dehydration—which leads to failure of the body's temperature control system. The medical definition of heat stroke is a core body temperature greater than 105°F, with complications involving the central nervous system that occur after exposure to high temperatures. Other common symptoms include nausea, seizures, confusion, disorientation, and, sometimes, loss of consciousness or coma.

Dehydration can lead to other potentially lethal complications. The Mayo Clinic[1] offers the following examples:

- **Seizures:** Electrolytes—such as potassium and sodium—help carry electrical signals from cell to cell. If your electrolytes are out of balance, the normal electrical messages can become mixed up, which can lead to involuntary muscle contractions, and, sometimes, loss of consciousness.
- **Low blood volume (hypovolemic shock):** This is one of the most serious, and sometimes life-threatening, complications of dehydration. It occurs when low blood volume

---

1   http://www.mayoclinic.org/diseases-conditions/dehydration/basics /complications/con-20030056.

causes a drop in blood pressure and a drop in the amount of oxygen in your body.

- **Swelling of the brain (cerebral edema):** Sometimes, when you're taking in fluids again after being dehydrated, the body tries to pull too much water back into your cells. This can cause some cells to swell and rupture. The consequences are especially grave when brain cells are affected.
- **Kidney failure:** This potentially life-threatening problem occurs when your kidneys are no longer able to remove excess fluids and waste from your blood.
- **Coma and death:** When not treated promptly and appropriately, severe dehydration can be fatal.

HOW TO TREAT DEHYDRATION

People who are suffering from dehydration must replace fluids and electrolytes. The most common way to do this is through oral rehydration therapy (ORT). In extreme cases, fluids must be given intravenously. In a disaster situation, hospitals may not be readily available, so every effort should be made to prevent the situation from reaching that level of severity.

Humans cannot survive without electrolytes, which are minerals in your blood and other bodily fluids that carry an electric charge. They are important because they are what your cells (especially those in your nerves, heart, and muscles) use to maintain voltages across cell membranes and to carry electrical impulses (nerve impulses and muscle contractions) across themselves and to other cells. Electrolytes, especially sodium, also help your body maintain its water balance.

Water itself does not contain electrolytes, but dehydration can cause serious electrolyte imbalances. In most situations, avoid giving the dehydrated person salt tablets because fresh, cool water is the best cure. In extreme temperatures or after very strenuous activities, electrolyte replacement drinks can be given. Sports drinks such as Gatorade can help replenish lost electrolytes. For children, rehydration beverages like Pedialyte can be helpful.

For electrolyte replacement, try this recipe:

- 2 liters water
- 10 tsp sugar (or artificial sweetener to taste if you can't use sugar)
- 1 tsp sea salt
- 1 tsp baking soda
- ½ teaspoon salt substitute (potassium salt)
- 1 pack sugar-free drink mix flavoring

Mix the ingredients until they are well-dissolved and drink to combat dehydration.

Store lots of water.

One of the best ways to avoid heat-related problems is to store lots of water. You can't always rely on the faucet in the kitchen. In the event of a disaster, the water may not run from the taps, and if it does, it might not be safe to drink, depending on the situation. If there is a boil order in place, remember that if the power is out, boiling your water may not be as easy as turning on your stove. If you are on a well and don't have a backup in place, you won't have running water.

Each family should store a two-week supply of water. The rule of thumb for drinking water is one gallon per day, per person. Don't forget to stock water for your pets also. See Appendix 3 (pg. 157) for more information on creating your water supply.

Keep cool during the blackout.

This is easier said than done when it's 105°F and you can't even run a ceiling fan. Here are some suggestions on keeping your house cool naturally that will help in the event of a power outage:

- **Channel your inner Southern belle.** Slowly fan yourself with a handheld fan. Mint juleps are optional.

- **Keep hydrated.** Your body needs the extra water to help produce sweat, which cools you off.
- **Change your schedule.** There's a reason that people who live near the equator close down their businesses and enjoy a midday siesta. Take a tepid shower and then, without drying off, lie down and try to take a nap. At the very least, do a quiet activity.
- **Play in the water.** Either place a kiddie pool in a shaded part of the yard or use the bathtub indoors. Find a nearby creek or pond for wading or swimming. (Note: Playing in the water isn't just for kids!)
- **Soak your feet.** A foot bath full of tepid water can help cool you down.
- **Avoid heavy meals**. Your body has to work hard to digest heavy, rich meals, and this raises your temperature. Be gentle on your system with light, cool meals, such as salads, cold soups, and fruit.
- **Make sure your screens are in good condition.** You're going to need to have your windows open, but fighting off insects when you're trying to sleep is a miserable and frustrating endeavor.
- **Invest in some battery-operated fans.** Particularly if you get yourself wet first, these little fans can help provide some real relief from the heat.

Be very conscious of food safety.

Food safety is always a concern if a power outage lasts for more than four hours, but it's even more likely you'll have food spoil during a hot weather blackout. You need to err on the side of caution in regard to refrigerated and frozen food. Coolers can help; you can put your most expensive perishables in a cooler and fill it with ice from the freezer to extend its lifespan. Whatever you do, open the doors to the refrigerator and freezer as infrequently as possible. This will help it maintain a cooler temperature for a longer time.

One DIY way to make sure your freezer food has remained at a safe temperature is to completely freeze a gallon of water, then place a penny on top and screw on the lid. If the penny sinks, you know that your freezer dropped below the freezing point, and if it stays at the top, things remained frozen.

According to the Red Cross,[2] if your freezer is half-filled and is not opened the entire time that the power is out, the food in it will remain sufficiently frozen for up to twenty-four hours. If it is completely filled, your food should remain safe for up to forty-eight hours. If the worst happens and your freezer full of meat does spoil, keep in mind that most homeowner's and renter's insurance policies will pay for their replacement, but unless you've lost a whole lot, or your deductible is very small, it may not be worth making a claim.

I strongly recommend the purchase of a digital, instant-read thermometer. This has many kitchen uses, but in the event of a disaster is worth its weight in gold for determining food safety. You can use your thermometer with the food safety chart in Appendix 9 (pg. 201) to determine the safety of your food.

Another way to combat the potential losses of a long-term summer power outage is to use other methods for preserving your food. Canning and dehydration are not grid-dependent and can save you a whole lot of money and prevent a mess of rotting meat in your freezer.

If a power outage looks like it's going to last for quite some time, you can be proactive if you have canning supplies on hand and a high-quality propane burner by pressure canning your meat outdoors to preserve it. Be very careful to supervise the canning pot; you don't want the pressure to drop to an unsafe level, and you want to keep kids and pets away from this project.

---

2   http://www.redcross.org/prepare/disaster/food-safety.

The rest of it is the same as prepping for any other power outage.

Many preparedness concerns are the same, no matter what time of year your power outage occurs. Here are some of the basic things you need for any power outage:

Appendix 2: Emergency Food Basics (pg. 151)

Appendix 3: Emergency Water Basics (pg. 157)

Appendix 4: Power Outage Survival Basics (pg. 167)

Appendix 6: Emergency Sanitation Basics (pg. 185)

Appendix 9: Food Safety Basics (pg. 201)

Appendix 10: Entertainment Basics (pg. 205)

Chapter 6

HOW TO SURVIVE A WILDFIRE EVACUATION

A few years ago, my family and I came very close to having to evacuate from a California wildfire, and by close, I mean two miles from disaster. The King Fire was a forest fire that nearly reached one hundred thousand acres.

We got up on a sunny Saturday morning, never realizing that would be the day an angry man would punctuate a domestic dispute by setting fire to a tree in the other person's yard. Certainly, no one expected one act of anger to set off a fire that would exceed the size of the city of Atlanta. However, he did set that fire, and it came within two miles from our home over the almost-two-weeks that we watched with bated breath.[1]

In the forested mountains of California, wildfires are an annual threat, and we've learned a lot about emergency evacuations, including how to be ready to roll in mere minutes. The speed at which you can get ready to move is key, because in some fast-moving disasters, seconds count.

The fall of 2017 was another horrible cautionary tale. As fire swept through the Napa region of California, forty-two people died,

1 https://www.theorganicprepper.com/the-king-fire-chronicles-life -on-the-edge-of-a-natural-disaster/.

8,400 structures were destroyed, and more than a billion dollars' worth of damage occurred.[2]

Wildfire evacuation isn't as easy as simply hopping in the car and leaving.
A lot of folks are critical of people's responses to a wildfire, saying blithely, "They knew there was a fire. They should have evacuated." It's important to understand that it doesn't always work like that with wildfires. Armchair quarterbacking is easy. Fleeing when the car you're driving literally *catches on fire* and the smoke is blinding you is not easy.

First of all, fires move rapidly. You can be in no danger whatsoever and just see a fire on the distant horizon, and then minutes later, it's at your back door. Second, they change course. Many times, the fire gets ahold of some new fuel like a home, tall grass, or trees, and the course veers in that direction. Finally, high winds have propelled these fires rapidly and fanned them to new heights. Every fall, California has something called the "Diablo Winds." These are seasonal gusts that can reach as high as 80 mph and cause extremely high fire danger. When coupled with existing fires, it's nothing less than the perfect storm.

In situations like this, there is often little to no warning before the fire is roaring through your property. The fire may be miles away and heading in the opposite direction one minute, then turn on a dime. Then suddenly, you find yourself directly in the path of an inferno. If you're lucky, you escape unscathed with your life but lose all your worldly possessions. Many people have not been lucky.

THINGS TO REMEMBER DURING A WILDFIRE
Bug-out bags are absolutely the first prep you should make. If you're just getting started, do this one thing. You can do

---

2   https://www.motherjones.com/environment/2017/10/california -fires-damage-total/.

it without spending a penny, by just gathering up things that you already own. You may not have a top of the line, "ready for the apocalypse" bag, but you'll still be far ahead of most people. When we first learned of the fire and realized that evacuating might become necessary, I had only two things to do. I had to get documents from the safe (the documents, by the way, were already housed in a plastic folder, so I only had to grab that one thing) and pull the pet carriers out of the shed. In less than five minutes, we were ready to roll. Had it been necessary, we could have left with only the photocopies of the documents, because those always remain in our bug-out bags. Having your bug-out bag ready means that you have accepted in advance that disaster could strike.

Any time one disaster strikes, several more are sure to follow. This is highly probable. Some people in the fire zone not only stayed on the edge of evacuation for nearly two weeks, but they also lost power due to the fire. This greatly reduced their ability to get news and information, which is vital in a rapidly changing disaster situation. It leads to even more worry and stress, and while you're dealing with the potential of your home burning down, you're also living through a power outage lasting several days. Getting prepared for a power outage (see Appendix 4 on page 167) is absolutely vital and can see you through most regional disasters.

Also, when it finally began to rain, although it helped to quench the flames, firefighters were suddenly threatened by flash floods and mudslides. These were made worse because the areas no longer had the same natural obstructions to deter the flow of water.

Get organized. All the lists in the world won't help you pack quickly if you don't know where things are. All of the items we deemed precious enough to pack and take with us are now stored in one area so that we won't have to look for them when seconds count.

You can't be prepared for everything. Disaster situations are always fluid, and they don't go by a script. It's vital to be adaptable to the changing situation.

Keep your vehicle full of fuel. If you have to evacuate, lots of other people will be hitting the road too. When you're stuck in traffic, you don't want to be worried about your fuel gauge dropping to the empty mark, leaving you stranded in a dangerous situation.

CREATE A SIMPLE FIRE KIT FOR YOUR VEHICLE

If you live in a fire-prone area, you need a fire kit in your vehicle at all times. Some things to include:

- **Swimming goggles:** This will protect your eyes and help keep you from being blinded by smoke.
- **Respirator masks:** This doesn't mean you will be able to breathe if the fire sucks all the oxygen from your environment, but it will help to filter out some of the smoke so you aren't disabled by a coughing fit.
- **Fire extinguisher:** In a worst-case scenario, if your vehicle catches on fire you may be able to put it out if you attack while the blaze is small.
- **Welding gloves:** It's easy to burn your hands opening a gate or moving debris from the road so you can get through. Welding gloves will offer some protection from hot surfaces.

Those items seem kind of unusual, but you'll be glad you have them if you ever have to drive through a fire zone.

TIPS FOR WILDFIRE EVACUATION

These are some other things I learned living in a wildfire zone and observing fires for the past five years.

- **Do *not* wait for the official order:** Often, after a wildfire, people are questioning why an evacuation alert never came. While officials do their best, *you* are the person who is responsible for your family's safety.

- **Have more than one escape route:** During a wildfire, you will sometimes find your escape route is blocked. Have more than one way out. Figure these routes out ahead of time and not when you are fleeing for your life and blinded by smoke.

- **Evacuate large animals ahead of time:** If possible, evacuate your livestock before the emergency becomes a crisis. In a situation like this, animals can be fearful and uncooperative. Get your livestock to safety first, because if you have to rush out like some families do, you'll have to leave them behind, helpless.

- **Leash or crate pets early on:** They will be affected by the same kind of panic as humans. A normally well-behaved pet could rush off into danger, leaving you to make the choice to leave them behind or risk your family's lives trying to save them.

- **Grab your dirty clothes hampers:** If you have time to grab a few things (unless you have just done laundry) grab dirty clothes hampers. They're likely to have several days of clothing from the skin out, PJs, and socks, saving you the time of searching for all those things individually.

- **Keep precious items and documents in one area:** Make sure irreplaceable things are kept together. We have a decorative trunk near the door in which we can sweep precious mementos. Important documents are backed up in the Cloud, which means we don't have to spend time packing those.

Remember, well before time to leave:

- Check your bug-out bags.
- Organize your most precious belongings.

- Discuss the plan with your family so that everyone knows what to expect.

In the event of a wildfire evacuation, your goal is to get out with your life. If you survive, you succeeded.

References for wildfire season:
Appendix 4: Power Outage Survival Basics (pg. 167)
Appendix 5: Evacuation Basics (pg. 173)
Appendix 7: Vehicle Emergency Kit Basics (pg. 193)

Chapter 7

HOW TO SURVIVE
A PANDEMIC

If the news announced tomorrow that a pandemic had begun and that your area in particular was at risk, would you be prepared?

It was only a couple of years ago that Ebola arrived on the shores of the United States. By sheer luck (certainly not by a well-managed response), the virus was contained. I had been prepping for quite some time, and had dealt with lengthy power outages, winter storms, and nearby forest fires with aplomb. When Patient Zero was diagnosed in Dallas, I realized that out of all of the things I was prepared for, a pandemic was not one of them. Sure, I'd have been better off than people who were completely unprepared, but I was lacking some vital supplies.

There is usually a little bit of warning before an outbreak becomes severe enough to warrant the title "pandemic." It isn't like *The Walking Dead*, where suddenly 80 percent of the population is affected overnight. With a pandemic, you hear a little hum about it before it gets bad. The World Health Organization makes some flyers, reports are given, and there is a mention on the evening news. But, generally speaking, officials are stingy with information because they don't want to "start a panic." This means that the judicious prepper needs to pay close attention when new viruses begin to be mentioned.

Now, just because a virus is mentioned, doesn't mean that it's going to become a pandemic, of course. However, it can be an early warning sign that you need to get your ducks in a row. Think of it like a tropical storm. You hear about it gathering steam out over the ocean well before it ever makes landfall. Just because there is a storm somewhere in the Atlantic doesn't mean that it's going to hit; it means that the wise person begins to pay closer attention to the weather reports, makes certain that the basics are stockpiled, and puts together a plan just in case the time to board up the windows arrives.

Let's talk about how easily a pandemic can spread in this day and age.

I'll use a more recent outbreak of Ebola as an example. Remember the soothing words of the World Health Organization about the Ebola outbreak in the Congo? Don't worry, they said. It's in a remote village that doesn't even have real roads, they said.

Except, the problem is, people began fleeing from that village in fear of the virus.[1]

> *KINSHASA, Democratic Republic of Congo: Ebola drove Kevin Balenge, his wife, and three children to get to this capital city as fast as they could to try to outrun a suspected new outbreak.*
>
> *"We can't stay here because there are no hospitals, and once you get the virus you simply die," said Balenge, from Bas-Uele province in the north of the country, about fifty-one hours away from Kinshasa.*
>
> *"Residents are still not aware of the virus and they do not know the precautions (to take)," he added. "Very many people are going to die here."*
>
> *... "Staying here is like trying to play with death," he said. "Ebola gives no second chance and I can't risk it. If I can save myself, I will try to do so."*

---

1   https://www.usatoday.com/story/news/world/2017/05/19/residents-flee
    -suspected-cases-ebola-outbreak-congo-grow/101879112/.

Now, we don't know if this family of five was infected or not, but the spread through Lakiti had increased exponentially at the time. Here are the facts.

- They traveled for fifty-one hours.
- They clearly made stops along the way in public places like gas stations, restaurants, restrooms, maybe motels.
- They would have paid for products and services, giving money to people who would, in turn, be in physical contact with other travelers.

After all that, the family ended up in the capital, where the population is about 8 million people.[2]

And that isn't even the worst of it.

In Kinshasa, there are many opportunities for even further transit, and fairly easily. It's where N'Djili International Airport is served by Kenya Airways, Air Zimbabwe, South African Airways, Ethiopian Airlines, Brussels Airlines, Air France, and Turkish Airlines, to name just a few. Where a person can fly to anywhere else in the world. Where a person could hop on a train or a boat at one of the country's largest ports and leave the country. Because of the ease of transit, the original carriers of the virus wouldn't need to be the ones leaving the country. They could stay right where they are and infect a person who is there visiting and who will soon get on a plane, train, or a boat and take the virus with them.

You see where I'm going with this. It's like watching the movie *Contagion*, except this is real. This is how easily a localized epidemic can turn into a global disaster. With anything deadly, whether it is Ebola, SARS, H1N1, MERS, H3N2, or an avian flu, the ease of travel and slow responses mean that these things can turn into pandemics. Adding panic to the mix is like throwing gasoline on a fire. They could even evolve into something along the lines of the

---

2   http://worldpopulationreview.com/countries/dr-congo-population/.

Spanish Influenza in 1918, which killed an estimated one hundred million people—and that happened well before we all began jet setting all over the place just for fun.

This doesn't even touch on the potential for a biological attack, something that more and more people are sounding the alarm about. A biological attack could be delivered by drone, or even by a person who has been deliberately infected. In his book *Failures of Imagination,* Congressman Michael McCaul of the Homeland Security Committee described possible terror threats against America. One of the potential scenarios depicted some women who had deliberately infected themselves with smallpox, then went to Disney World in order to reach people who would be going home to places all across the country, quickly spreading a deadly illness.

You need to know what you're dealing with.
You will have to make adjustments based on variables like how the virus is transmitted, how it is treated, the course the illness takes, and the virulence and mortality rate. Well before an outbreak occurs, you'll want to have information on hand that will help you to plan efficiently. The book I recommend for this is *Prepping for a Pandemic* by Cat Ellis. This guide breaks down a number of different potential pandemics. You can use it ahead of time to help make your plans, and in the event of a pandemic, you already possess this vital information.

PANDEMIC LOCKDOWN
In the event of an illness that has a high death count, one of the most basic ways to avoid catching the illness is to go into lockdown. Avoiding contact with people who have the illness is the only way to prevent infection. Isolating your family is the best way to stay safe and healthy. It's low-tech, doesn't require an untested vaccination, and it's highly effective.

This isn't something most of us would be willing or able to do in ordinary circumstances, of course. Few of us can pull the kids from school, stay home from work, and refuse to open the door to the UPS guy for a period of six to eight weeks. To make a move so extreme, the concern wouldn't be about contracting an ordinary virus, it would be about a serious, life-threatening contagion.

If the situation hits close enough to home that you decide it's time to isolate yourselves, the rules to this are intractable:

No one goes out. No one comes in.

I know this sounds harsh, but there are to be no exceptions. If you make exceptions, you might as well go wrestle with runny-nosed strangers at the local Wal-Mart and then come home and hug your children, because it's the same thing.

Once you have gone into lockdown mode, that means that the supplies you have on hand are the supplies you have to see you through. You can't run out to the store and get something you've forgotten. That means if a family member shows up, they have to go into quarantine for at least four weeks (more or less, depending on the specifics of the disease), during which time they are not allowed access to the home or family, nor are they allowed to go out in public. If it is likely that some people will show up, set up an area on your property that is far from your home for them to hang out for their month of quarantine. If at the end of the month they are presenting no symptoms, then they can come in. Sadly, it also means that you may be forced to turn someone away if they are ill, because to help them means to risk your family.

When should you go into lockdown?

This is the tricky part: How do you know that the time has come to get the family inside and lock the doors behind you? Lizzie Bennett, a retired medical professional, wrote an incredibly helpful article on her website Underground Medic.[3]

Bennett recommends social distancing as the only effective way to protect yourself and your family from an outbreak of disease.

---

3   http://undergroundmedic.com/.

How long you should remain isolated depends primarily on where you live. For those in towns and cities it will be for much longer than those living in rural retreats where human contact is minimal. Though those fortunate enough to live in such surroundings should remember that if the situation is dire enough, people will leave the cities looking for safety in less populated areas.

In large centers of population there will be more people moving around, legally or otherwise, each of these individuals represents a possible uptick in the disease rates, allowing the spread to continue longer than it would have they stayed indoors and/or out of circulation.

Even when the initial phase is on the wane, or has passed through an area, people travelling into that area can bring it back with them triggering a second wave of disease as people are now emerging from their isolation . . .

. . . One hundred miles is my buffer zone for disease, of course it could already be in my city, but practicalities dictate that I will not stay away from people because hundreds in Europe are dropping like flies. Maps of disease spread look like a locust swarm moving across the country and this allows disease spread to be tracked on an hour by hour basis. One of the few instances where mainstream media will be useful.

Once you've gone into lockdown, how long you must stay there is dependent on the spread of the illness, the type of illness, and other factors. Times will vary. Bennett suggests these guidelines:

Once the doors were locked we would stay there for at least two weeks after the last case within 100 miles is reported. A government all clear would be weighed against how long it had been since the last case was reported in the area I have designated as my buffer zone. There is of course still the chance that someone from outside the area will bring the disease in with them causing a second wave of illness. You cannot seal off cities to prevent this.

Going out after self-imposed isolation should be kept to a minimum for as long as possible, and if you don't have to, then don't do it. Far

HOW TO SURVIVE A PANDEMIC   53

*better to let those that are comfortable being out and about get on with it
and see if any new cases emerge before exposing yourself and your family
to that possibility.*

Before a pandemic is even on the local radar is the time to plan with
your preparedness group (or your individual family) how you intend
to handle the situation.

- Will you shelter together, in the same location?
- Will you reserve a secondary location to retreat to if the situation worsens further or if someone becomes ill?
- Will you shelter separately because of the nature of the emergency?
- What event and proximity will trigger you to go into lockdown mode?

Make your plan and stick to it, regardless of pressure from those
who think you are overreacting, the schools that your children have
stopped attending, and any other external influences. If you've
decided there is a great enough risk that you need to go into lockdown, you must adhere to your plan.

What supplies do you need when prepping for a pandemic?
When preparing for anything, you must have the basic items in
order to care for your family for a length of time without leaving
the house, and pandemics are no different. But with a pandemic,
there are other supplies you'd need that you may not have on hand.
You'll want to be able to create an isolation area for potentially ill
family members, have supplies on hand to care for people safely if
they do become ill, and the necessary tools to prevent the spread of
the illness through the household. It's most likely that services such
as public water and electricity will remain intact, but you should
prepare as though they won't be, just in case. (See Appendix 4 on
page 167.)

Here's a quick pandemic readiness checklist:

- Food (See Appendix 2 on page 151)
- Drinking water (See Appendix 3 on page 157)
- Heavy duty garbage bags for biological waste (the 3 mL thick contractor type is the best)
- Sanitation supplies (See Appendix 6 on page 185)
- Entertainment (See Appendix 10 on page 205)
- Basic medical supplies (See Appendix 8 on page 197)
- Extra N95 masks
- N100 masks
- Nitrile gloves
- Safety goggles with an elastic band to ensure a snug fit
- Protective clothing, preferably Tyvek
- Antibacterial cleaners such as disposable wipes, bleach, and spray cleaners
- Antibacterial hand sanitizer

(Note: even if you don't commonly use antibacterial products, in a pandemic situation, it's important to have this type of thing on hand.)

Prepare an isolation area.
In the event that a member of your group becomes ill, they need to immediately be quarantined from the rest of the group. By the time they're showing symptoms, it could be too late to prevent the spread of illness, but an effort should still be taken to isolate them.

Here are some tips on isolating a patient:

- The sick room should be sealed off from the rest of the house. Use a heavy tarp over the doorway to the room on the inside and the outside. This will make a small breezeway for the caretaker to go in and out.

- The caretaker should cover up with disposable clothing, gloves, shoe covers, and hair covers.
- The caretaker should wear an N95 mask.
- The sick person should use disposable dishes and cutlery. All garbage from the sick room should be placed in a heavy garbage bag and burned outdoors immediately.
- The sick person should not leave the room. If there is not a bedroom with a connected bathroom, a bathroom setup should be created within the room. Great care must be taken with the disposal of this waste.

Prevention is the best, and sometimes only, option for survival in the event of a deadly pandemic.

Chapter 8

HOW TO SURVIVE A NUCLEAR DISASTER

Learning what to do in the event of a nuclear strike has recently taken on a whole new urgency with foreign governments hinting at the possibility of nuking the United States. Even the CDC has warned Americans to get prepared for the possibility of nuclear war.[1]

A nuclear attack could mean one of two things: a missile sent to some location on American soil or an electromagnetic pulse (EMP) that detonated above the country, wiping out the power grid. If that isn't enough of a threat, there are ninety-nine nuclear facilities in our country, any of which could be subject to some type of disaster. Many of the suggestions that follow will also apply in the event of a nuclear meltdown. Preparing for a strike versus an EMP are very different. For the purposes of this guide, we'll talk about a direct strike.

Would a nuclear attack kill us all or cause a global nuclear winter?

I got a message from a reader during the North Korean nuclear crisis that encompassed what a lot of people were thinking:

> N. Korea now has a Nuke or Nuke capabilities. Do you beef up your preps, wait for the chips to fall, kiss your butt goodbye, or other? Should we be acting business as usual?

---

1   https://www.theorganicprepper.com/cdc-warns-americans-nuclear-war/.

First, let me dispel two myths about a nuclear attack.

We won't all die or wish we were dead if a nuclear strike occurs. The movies, as much as I love them, have done us a terrible disservice here. If you are at Ground Zero of an attack, there is absolutely nothing you can do. Everything will be vaporized and that's that. However, if you are outside the immediate blast zone, it is completely survivable, and I don't mean survivable in the horrible, lingering death kind of way. I mean, unharmed. You just have to know exactly what to do *immediately* in order to protect yourself. More on that in a moment.

We won't suffer a nuclear winter. Everyone thinks it will be like the post-apocalyptic scenario in that horribly inaccurate book/movie, *The Road*. In that particular plot, the nuclear war was so great that a huge cloud of ash covered the planet. In reality, it would take *hundreds* of nuclear strikes to cause something like that, which is unlikely to occur. This isn't to downplay the horror and death of one strike, but to point out that the aftermath isn't going to make the quality of life on Earth as terrible as what the movies portray. Contrary to popular belief, a nuke won't kill everyone within hundreds of miles. If you aren't in the immediate blast radius, a nuclear strike is absolutely survivable. The one-mile radius around the blast will be virtually un-survivable. Within two miles, people will suffer third degree burns from the intense wave of heat. If you are within two miles of the blast, the winds will be coming at about six hundred miles per hour. This will take down buildings and cause a tremendous amount of pressure. Some experts recommend that you keep your mouth open to try and reduce the tremendous pressure on your eardrums. Also, resist the urge to stare in horror. Looking at the blast could cause permanent blindness.

According to the DHS, ten kilotons is the approximate size of nuclear weapon we could expect. Here's what that would look like:[2]

- Nearly everyone within a half-mile radius of the point of impact would die and most of the buildings would be demolished. This would be considered Ground Zero.
- The area within the next half mile would suffer extensive damage, fires, and serious injuries.
- Areas within three miles could see minor injuries to people and slight damage to their homes.
- The fallout would kill even more people. According to the DHS:
  - Within ten to twenty miles of the explosion, radioactive exposure would cause nausea and vomiting in mere hours and death without medical treatment.
  - But for those near enough to the blast, experiencing more than 800R of radiation, not seeking shelter immediately would cause deaths with or without medical treatment, the study found.
  - People *would not* be able to evacuate this area as fallout would arrive within just ten minutes.

People upwind of the strike and outside the twenty-mile radius would be unlikely to suffer any effects. People downwind would need to take shelter. Deaths from cancer that are related to the fallout could occur for many years after.

Here's how an average family can prep for a nuclear attack.
As cool as it would be to have one, you don't have to have a bunker to survive if you take the time now to get prepped. You can

---

2   http://www.dailymail.co.uk/sciencetech/article-3194437/We-not-prepared -Scientist-reveals-terrifying-vision-happen-America-hit-nuclear-bomb .html.

survive by learning everything you can to prepare for a nuclear attack.

So, here's what I'm doing. Every time a new threat rolls around, I discover that while I have many of my bases covered, there are a few things I hadn't accounted for. A nuclear threat is no different. There were some supplies I had to pick up myself, particularly a bigger supply of no-cook food.

Part of your preparations will depend on where you live, so this will be different for everyone. Are you near any places that are likely targets? Places like Washington DC, Hawaii, New York City, Los Angeles, and large military bases are more likely targets than, say, a low population area in the Midwest. Of course, this doesn't mean it can't happen, just that it's less likely.

Are you in a house or an apartment building? What is the best place in your home to seek shelter? Plan all of this ahead of time. If you know exactly what steps you are going to take, you will be able to better perform them under pressure.

Here are some key points to consider:

You won't have a whole lot of notice. Scientists say that residents of Hawaii might have only eight to twelve minutes notice if an ICBM was headed their way, and residents of New York City could have an hour. Clearly, there won't be time to run to the store, and if you did, you'd be fighting it out with a bunch of panicked people, so get your supplies together *now*.

You could be in your car. If you are in your car, make certain to turn the vent to recirculation so that you don't bring any outside air into the vehicle. Your goal should be to immediately get to shelter.

Be prepared to go into lockdown. In nearly every case, staying home is the best course of action. Imagine you are in New York City and this nuke is headed your way. If you try to evacuate, you are likely to get stuck on one of the bridges on the way out of Manhattan.

That would be far deadlier than hunkering down in your apartment and hoping you are outside the half mile radius of Ground Zero. Experts say that you should plan to stay sheltered for a minimum of nine days. My personal plan is two to three weeks, depending on proximity and wind direction. I'd rather err on the side of caution.

Professor Irwin Redlener,[3] a specialist on disaster preparedness, discussed what to do immediately during a talk on nuclear preparedness:

> In that 10 to 15 minutes, all you have to do is go about a mile away from the blast.
>
> Within 20 minutes, it comes straight down. Within 24 hours, lethal radiation is going out with prevailing winds.
>
> You've got to get out of there. If you don't get out of there, you're going to be exposed to lethal radiation in very short order.
>
> If you can't get out of there, we want you to go into a shelter and stay there. Now, in a shelter in an urban area means you have to be either in a basement as deep as possible, or you have to be on a floor—on a high floor—if it's a ground burst explosion, which it would be, higher than the ninth floor.
>
> So you have to be tenth floor or higher, or in the basement. But basically, you've got to get out of town as quickly as possible. And if you do that, you actually can survive a nuclear blast.
>
> The most hazardous fallout particles are readily visible as fine sand-sized grains so you must keep away from them and not go outside if you see them.

SURVIVAL SHELTER CHECKLIST

There are two things for which people would need to prepare: the blast and the fallout.

---

3   http://www.mirror.co.uk/news/uk-news/world-war-3-how-you
    —6904856.

No one *wants* to think about this kind of thing, but it's oh-so-important. Keep in mind that a survival shelter doesn't have to be a "bunker" in the traditional sense. (Although how awesome would that be?) It could be your basement, an interior room in the house, a room with fewer windows and access points, or a room that you can harden if necessary. If there is absolutely no place in your home where you can shelter, find out if the town where you reside has a public fallout or blast shelter.

The goal is to put as much *mass* between you and the outside air as possible. The ideal amount is three feet. Windows are not an acceptable barrier. But *do not* let a situation that is less than ideal overwhelm you to the point that you don't take the steps you can. Very few of us have a concrete underground bunker with no windows. Very few of us have an unlimited budget. Start with the basics and add the things you can, when you can.

Answer the following questions:

- Where would you take shelter for fourteen to twenty-one days?
- Do you have the necessary supplies to fortify your shelter? (Duct tape, heavy plastic, boards, or sandbags to seal off windows, doors, vents, and any other place where a draft can get through.)
- Is the shelter stocked with enough food for you to wait for the radiation to dissipate? (See Appendix 2 on page 151.)
- Do you have a way to safely cook food? Alternatively, do you have foods that don't require cooking? (See Appendix 2 on page 151.)
- Do you have blankets and comfort items?
- Do you have enough water for everyone? (See Appendix 3 on page 157.)
- Do you have potassium iodide, and do you know how to take it? (Instructions to follow.)
- How would you use the bathroom in your shelter? (See Appendix 6 on page 185.)

- How would your pets do their business? (Puppy pads? Newspaper? Litter box?)
- Do you have enough pet food?
- Do you have supplies for special needs like diapers, formula, medications, comfort items?
- Do you have something for people to do while you shelter in place? (See Appendix 10 on page 205.)

After you answer these questions, it's time to go deeper into your plan.

Fortify your home against fallout.

As I mentioned before, your goal is to put as much mass as possible between you and the radioactive fallout. Mass should be as dense and thick as possible.

- Use duct tape and tarps to seal off all windows, doors, and vents. Get a *lot* of duct tape and tarps.
- Then add mass of any type you can get your hands on. Sandbags are a good way to quickly create mass. Take shelter in a basement if possible and fortify the windows and doors with as much mass as possible.
- Turn off any type of climate control that pulls the outside air into your home. Expect to survive without heat or air conditioning for the duration.
- Close off your chimney.
- If someone enters the home, make certain that there is a room set up that is separate from other family members so that they can decontaminate. All clothing they were wearing should be placed outside and they should immediately shower thoroughly.
- Make a breezeway for putting things outdoors (like pet or human waste). Hang heavy tarps around the door and put on disposable coveralls, gloves, shoe covers, and masks if

you have to actually go out. Disrobe, discard the disposable clothing by tossing it out the door, and shower immediately when you get back inside.

- If you don't have a basement, go to the most central part of your house and erect as many barriers as possible. If there is no central area without windows and exterior walls, go to the room furthest away from prevailing winds.

Have enough supplies on hand to wait out the danger.

As with many emergencies, you need to be prepared to survive at home without help from anyone. It's unknown whether water and electricity will be running, and if the water is running, whether it will be safe to drink. Prep as though you won't have access to these utilities and then if you do, it'll be a pleasant surprise.

- Stock up on emergency food. If your emergency cooking methods rely on being able to go outdoors, focus on no-cook foods that do not require refrigeration. Canned vegetables and fruits, canned beans, pouches of rice and quinoa, crackers, peanut butter, dried fruit. You get the idea. The eating may not be exciting, but you won't starve to death. Don't forget a supply of pet food. (See Appendix 2 on page 151.)
- Have a supply of water for all family members and pets that will last throughout the nine-day waiting period that you need to remain indoors. (Or longer, which is what we're planning.) (See Appendix 3 on page 157.)
- Get paper plates and cutlery in the event that the water isn't running so you don't have to waste your precious supply for washing dishes.
- Be prepared for potential power outage. (See Appendix 4 on page 167.)
- If you have pets, have supplies on hand for their sanitation. You can't let them go outside because not only would they be exposed, they would bring radiation in with them. So, pee

pads, cat litter, etc. are all necessary. Solid waste can probably be flushed.

- Have the supplies to create an emergency toilet for humans if you have no bathroom in your shelter of if the plumbing does not work. Stock hand sanitizer, bleach wipes, and baby wipes as well. (See Appendix 6 on page 185.)
- Make sure to have a supply of any necessary prescription medications that will last through the time that you hunker down.
- Have a well-stocked first aid kit. It's entirely likely that medical assistance will not be available, and if it is, you'll put yourself at risk by going out to seek it. (See Appendix 8 on page 197.)
- Have a way to receive news from the outside world. An emergency radio is a must. You can't count on the Internet or cell service to be available.

Learn everything you can about nuclear emergencies. The more you know, the better your chances are of surviving unscathed.

POTASSIUM IODIDE

This section explains how to use potassium iodide (KI) after a nuclear strike and addresses some frequently asked questions. I'm not a doctor. This article is based on research done on the FDA and CDC websites.

Why do you need potassium iodide after a nuclear emergency?

Aside from the immediate threats of a nuclear blast, the thyroid gland is the most susceptible organ to damage from radiation. Potassium iodide is a stable form of iodine (stable meaning it isn't radioactive). If the thyroid gland is loaded with stable iodine, it can't absorb radioactive iodine. Radioactive iodine can cause cancer. Here's how the CDC explains it:

The thyroid gland cannot tell the difference between stable and radioac-
tive iodine. It will absorb both.

KI (potassium iodide) blocks radioactive iodine from entering the
thyroid. When a person takes KI, the stable iodine in the medicine gets
absorbed by the thyroid. Because KI contains so much stable iodine,
the thyroid gland becomes "full" and cannot absorb any more iodine—
either stable or radioactive—for the next 24 hours.

This doesn't protect your body from any other type of radioactive
isotopes, only radioactive iodine. It won't undo the damage done
by radioactive iodine, so you must begin taking it immediately for
protection. If there is no radioactive threat, you should not take KI,
as it can be harmful.

How do you take potassium iodide after a nuclear strike or other radiation emergency?

The sooner you begin taking KI after an emergency, the better. It
works best if taken within three to four hours of an emergency.

Here are the dosages recommended by the CDC.[4]

- **Newborns from birth to 1 month of age** should be given 16 mg (¼ of a 65 mg tablet or ¼ mL of solution). This dose is for both nursing and non-nursing newborn infants.
- **Infants and children between 1 month and 3 years of age** should take 32 mg (½ of a 65 mg tablet or ½ mL of solution). This dose is for both nursing and non-nursing infants and children.
- **Children between 3 and 18 years** of age should take 65 mg (one 65 mg tablet or 1 mL of solution).
- **Children who are adult size (greater than or equal to 150 pounds)** should take the full adult dose, regardless of their age.

---

4 https://emergency.cdc.gov/radiation/ki.asp.

- **Adults** should take 130 mg (one 130 mg tablet OR two 65 mg tablets OR two mL of solution).
- **Women who are breastfeeding** should take the adult dose of 130 mg.

Here's a chart provided by the FDA:[5]

	Predicted Thyroid Gland exposure (cGy)	KI dose (mg)	Number or fraction of 130 mg tablets	Number or fraction of 65 mg tablets	Milliters (mL) of oral solution, 65 mg/mL***
Adults over 40 years	≥ 500	130	1	2	2 mL
Adults over 18 through 40 years	≥ 10	130	1	2	2 mL
Pregnant or lactating women	≥ 5	130	1	2	2 mL
Adolescents, 12 through 18 years	≥ 5	65	½	1	1 mL
Children over 3 years through 12 years	≥ 5	65	½	1	1 mL
Children 1 month through 3 years	≥ 5	32	Use KI oral solution**	½	0.5 mL
Infants birth through 1 month	≥ 5	16	Use KI oral solution**	Use KI oral solution**	0.25 mL

One full dose protects the thyroid gland for twenty-four hours. Taking more does not add more protection and can cause illness or death. During times of extended exposure, take the dose once every twenty-four hours for the length of time recommended by emergency officials. (You've got your battery-operated or hand crank emergency radio, right?)

---

5   https://www.fda.gov/Drugs/EmergencyPreparedness/Bioterrorismand DrugPreparedness/ucm072265.htm.

The following guidance is offered by the FDA:[6]

- The FDA guidance prioritizes groups based on age, which is the primary factor for determining risk for radioiodine-induced thyroid cancer.
- Those at highest risk are infants and children, as well as pregnant and nursing females because of the potential for KI to suppress thyroid function in the developing fetus and the newborn.
- The recommendation is to treat them at the lowest threshold (with respect to predicted radioactive dose to the thyroid).
- Anyone over 18 years old and up to 40 years old should be treated at a slightly higher threshold.
- Anyone over 40 years old should be treated with KI only if the predicted exposure is high enough to destroy the thyroid and induce lifelong hypothyroidism (thyroid deficiency).

Remember: Do *not* give infants, pregnant women, or breastfeeding women more than one dose of KI.

Who should *not* take potassium iodide?

Some people should not take KI because the risks outweigh the benefits. According to the FDA, the following people should not take KI:

- Persons with known iodine sensitivity
- Persons with allergies to iodine, iodide, and shellfish
- Individuals with dermatitis herpetiformis and hypocomplementemic vasculitis
- People with nodular thyroid with heart disease

---

6   https://www.fda.gov/Drugs/EmergencyPreparedness/Bioterrorism andDrugPreparedness/ucm072265.htm.

- Individuals with multinodular goiter, Graves' disease, and autoimmune thyroiditis should be treated with caution—especially if dosing extends beyond a few days. Speak to your doctor, because KI could be deadly for you.

A seafood or shellfish allergy does not necessarily mean that you are allergic or hypersensitive to iodine, but extreme caution should be used, and you should have the supplies on hand to treat a life-threatening allergic reaction. Personally, I probably would not take KI if I had a seafood allergy. If you are not sure if you should take KI, consult your healthcare professional before a disaster ever occurs.

If your thyroid gland has been removed, you will not benefit from taking KI.

What are the possible side effects of potassium iodide?

If you take the correct dosage and are not allergic to iodine, you shouldn't have any negative side effects. The possible issues are:

- Skin rashes
- Swelling of the salivary glands
- "Iodism" (metallic taste, burning mouth and throat, sore teeth and gums, symptoms of a head cold, and sometimes upset stomach and diarrhea)

An allergic reaction can have more serious symptoms. These include fever and joint pains; swelling of parts of the body (face, lips, tongue, throat, hands, or feet); trouble breathing, speaking, or swallowing; wheezing or shortness of breath. Severe shortness of breath requires immediate medical attention.

What kind of potassium iodide should I use for my emergency supplies?

Table salt, iodine-rich foods, and low-dose supplements do not contain enough iodine to be effective. If you live near a nuclear plant, you may be able to acquire an approved source of potassium iodide for your entire household, free of charge from the facility.

The FDA has approved these brands for use in a nuclear emergency. (I've included links to the products I could find.) The FDA recommends that you only take the following brands.

- iOSAT tablets, 130mg, from Anbex, Inc.
- ThyroSafe tablets, 65mg, from Recipharm AB (You'll have to pay extra for rush shipping of this brand to get it immediately)
- ThyroShield oral solution, 65mg/mL, from Arco Pharmaceuticals, LLC
- Potassium Iodide Oral Solution USP, 65mg/mL, from Mission Pharmacal Company

It's essential to note that if you use a non-approved product, it may not be as effective as FDA approved products. I strongly urge you to get the recommended brands if possible.

The following sources were used to compile this information:

- KI in Radiation Emergencies[7]
- Potassium Iodide as a Thyroid Blocking Agent in Radiation Emergencies[8]
- FDA[9]
- CDC[10]

You *can* survive if you prepare for a nuclear attack, so get prepared. Today. Because we just don't know what's about to happen.

---

7   https://www.fda.gov/downloads/Drugs/GuidanceCompliance RegulatoryInformation/Guidances/UCM080546.pdf.
8   https://www.fda.gov/downloads/Drugs/GuidanceCompliance RegulatoryInformation/Guidances/UCM080542.pdf.
9   https://www.fda.gov/drugs/emergencypreparedness/bioterrorismanddrug preparedness/ucm072265.htm.
10 https://emergency.cdc.gov/radiation/ki.asp.

Chapter 9

HOW TO SURVIVE
A MASS SHOOTING

When horrible events happen, people want to know why. Why was a random group of people targeted to have their innocent day destroyed by violence and terror? Why did the culprit choose that group of victims, that day on the calendar, that specific location? And who? Who was the mastermind behind the event? Who were the members of the group that perpetrated the horror?

These questions are always followed by the speculation that things are not as they have been presented to us. Most people in the preparedness world have a very valid mistrust of the corporate-sponsored mainstream media. We look to other sources for our news, and rightly so. That speculation includes accusations that our own government is behind it, pulling the strings. Other frequent theories are that the events never actually happened at all and that the victims are 100 percent made up of crisis actors.

The pursuit of the truth is an important quest. Some journalists have dedicated their entire lives to uncovering the Machiavellian plots of those who pull the strings, and it's a noble and meaningful calling. That is why what I'm about to say is controversial and probably won't be well-received by everyone who reads it.

It doesn't matter who is responsible.

Strictly from a survival point of view, it doesn't matter at all who committed the acts of terror that occurred on 9/11, on the streets of Boston, in London, at various schools across the country, in Las

Vegas, or in Paris. It doesn't matter whether the shooting at Sandy Hook was perpetrated by a kid with behavioral issues or by operatives with an agenda.

If your focus is preparedness and survival, the most important thing you can be doing right now is learning a lesson in survival from these events. This is not a debate about the different conspiracy theories. If you are present during a mass shooting, my opinions on the culprit don't matter and neither do yours. All that matters in those minutes or hours is surviving.

We'll talk about three types of events. A mass-shooting or terror attack that takes place close-up, a shooting that happens from a long distance, and a school shooting. Remember this, my friends. Right now, someone, somewhere, is making plans to kill you. Does it really matter who when the bullets start flying? Are you arguing over theories, or are you making plans to survive?

SURVIVING A MASS SHOOTING

The world has always been populated with those who seek power, attention, and control. Acts of terror are nearly always about one or all of those things, and mass shootings are nothing if not acts of terror. The perpetrators are predators and the victims are the prey. If you are a target of the first wave of the attack, there may not be a lot you can do about it. If you're hit in the back with gunfire, if you happen to be at a concert that is the target of a sniper, if you are going about your business and someone opens fire in the subway car you're in, there isn't a lot you can do.

If you are fortunate enough not to be a victim of the first wave, of an attack, you can survive. Often, before the first wave occurs, there are minute details that can tell you something is wrong. One of my favorite movies is *The Bourne Identity*. If you haven't seen it, despite Jason Bourne's amnesia, he possesses skills that are ingrained into his psyche. As a former operative, he was trained to be highly observant and to make rapid assessments of what he observed.

While most of us haven't been trained as operatives, we can still maintain a high level of situational awareness merely by being observant. One way to develop your skills is to play something called "Kim's Game." The game stems comes from *Kim*, a novel by Rudyard Kipling, and is something you can play with your family, anywhere, anytime.

My friend Scott of graywolfsurvival.com used to use the game to train his soldiers in situational awareness. He wrote:[1]

Situational awareness is key to understanding your environment, so you can know better both your circumstances and your options. There are myriad examples that could be given but would you notice the bulge (called printing) of someone's ankle from a concealed weapon if you were asked to follow him to barter for goods? Would you remember enough details of the turn of a path you passed two hours ago to be able to find it again? If you were attacked, would you be able to give a good enough description of the subject and get-away vehicle to have him identified?

A higher level of situational awareness can help you in many ways, should you be unfortunate enough to be present during an act of terror. It can help by:

- Allowing you to identify a threat before it becomes active
- Allowing you to locate exits and routes to the exits
- Allowing you to determine sources of cover

If you can identify a potential threat before it exists, you can some-times prevent an attack or at the very least protect yourself and your family more effectively. A book by Patrick Van Horne and Jason A. Riley describes the moments before something bad happens, when

---

1   http://graywolfsurvival.com/2173/using-kims-game-to-train-your-mind-for-survival/.

you have an inkling that something is wrong but you just can't put your finger on what it is, as being on the "left of bang."

The book, *Left of Bang: How the Marine Corps' Combat Hunter Program Can Save Your Life*, discusses how establishing a baseline can help you to identify a threat. I can't recommend this book enough. A baseline is a "normal" for your immediate environment. Once you have a baseline for behavior in a specific environment, it becomes easier to spot anomalies. According to *Left of Bang*, it's the anomalies that should put you on high alert. "Anomalies are things that either do not happen and should, or that do happen and shouldn't."

ACCEPTANCE IS THE FIRST STEP TO SURVIVING AN ATTACK

If you don't realize ahead of time that something horrible is going down, that doesn't mean that you won't survive. It's the actions you take immediately upon the realization that have the potential to save your life. When bullets start flying, you can't spend five minutes thinking, "This can't actually be happening." It *is* happening and moving past accepting that propels you through the first step into the second one.

The people who freeze in a mass shooting do nothing but make themselves easier targets. Freezing is an innate reaction for some people, but you can train your way through that. Training in self-defense, first aid, and disaster preparedness can help offset the brain's neurobiological response that leaves some people paralyzed with fear.

Think through scenarios well before they happen and solve problems before they occur. When you have a preparedness mind-set, you're one step ahead of those who never even considered the idea that something bad could happen.

THREE COURSES OF ACTION IN A MASS SHOOTING

We can't always predict when an attack is about to happen. There might be no indications in your immediate surroundings to alert you to the fact that something is amiss. You may be blithely unaware until the moment a gun is fired.

If you find yourself suddenly in the midst of an active shooting, your actions should be one of the following:

1. **Escape.** Get as far away from the threat as possible. This is where your early observant behavior comes in handy, because you'll already know the escape routes. If you are in charge of vulnerable individuals like children, your first choice of action should always be to get them to safety if at all possible.

2. **Take cover.** If you can't get away, get behind something solid and wait for your opportunity to either escape or fight back. This is something else you may have observed when doing your earlier reconnaissance. Remember, concealment hides you from the shooter, but doesn't protect you from bullets. Cover both hides you and protects you.

3. **Take out the threat**. If you are armed and/or trained, use your abilities to help remove the threat.

The most important thing to consider here is not necessarily which action you will take, but that you *will take an action*, and not just stand there in shock. You can be a victim or you can be a warrior.

In the Paris massacre, unarmed hostages were at the mercy of their captors. One hundred people were kept in line by just a few men with guns. Keep in mind that fighting back doesn't always mean a fancy Krav Maga move that takes down two armed men with one trick maneuver. There are many ways to fight back, and not all of them require physical prowess. Don't let fear incapacitate you. Your brain is a weapon, too.

Are you going to wait for someone to save you or are you going to save yourself? Don't be a *kamikaze* but look for your opportunity. There comes a point in some of these situations in which survival is unlikely. Don't go down without a fight.

You have to train.

As a wise friend pointed out, while a plan is important, you must train to be able to carry out your plan. If you don't have the fitness level or skills, you won't be able to accomplish what you're planning to do. Just because you could do it in high school doesn't mean you can do it now, thirty years later.

- Are you fit?
- Do you practice self-defense skills?
- Are you comfortable with your firearm in a variety of settings and applications?

If the answers to these questions are not "yes," all the planning in the world will be of little avail.

Always be ready for a second wave in the event of a terror attack.

Some people set on spreading terror are full of surprises. For example, in more than one case, after an initial attack of running a vehicle into a crowd of pedestrians, men armed with knives got out and began lashing. Explosives are also not outside the realm of possibility after a preliminary attack. Occasionally the attacks are carried out by a team and just when it looks like the primary attacker is down, others continue.

Evacuate the area as soon as possible to avoid getting injured or killed in the second wave. If you can't leave the area, be on high alert for anything else that looks "off" and be prepared to respond.

SURVIVING A LONG-DISTANCE SHOOTING

An entirely different set of rules applies when it comes to surviving a sniper attack or one where a shooter is safely stationed some distance away and spraying a crowd of people with gunfire. Of course, one of the most memorable and deadly of these events was the one that took place at an outdoor concert in Las Vegas, Nevada in 2017.

The thing with an event like the one in Las Vegas is that a great deal of your survival depends on nothing but luck. If you happen to be in the wrong place at the wrong time, skills won't necessarily save you.

The Las Vegas shooting was different than many previous mass shootings because the culprit was not directly in the thick of things. He was a sniper, 400 yards away from his target of 22,000 people attending a concert. Due to the shooter's distance, the standard advice of run, hide, or fight was completely useless. People had no idea where the shots were coming from, which meant they didn't know where to run. Hiding is not easy in a wide-open space, similar to a giant parking lot without the cars. You can't fight an enemy that far away. Even if you were a concealed carry permit holder who had brought your gun into a venue where you aren't "allowed" to have it, your carry firearm wouldn't shoot far enough, and identifying the threat from that distance while everyone is panicking would be all but impossible.

Because of the shooter's distance, none of the evasion techniques like running in a zig-zag pattern or getting down were likely to make a huge difference to a person so far away whose apparent goal was only to hurt or kill as many people as possible.

So, how do you survive a long-distance attack?
This is what I learned when researching a horror scenario like the Las Vegas massacre.

- **Know what gunfire sounds like.** A lot of people who were interviewed said that when they first heard the shots, they didn't realize what they were. They thought the sound was fireworks. There were precious seconds when people were frozen targets while they tried to wrap their brains around what was actually happening. During an event like this, a pause of a few seconds could mean the difference between life and death. The faster you take action the more likely you are to survive.

- **Always have a plan.** We can't foresee all eventualities like this one, for example, but it helps to always have a survival mindset. It has long been a game with my kids (yeah, we're a strange family) to identify exits and potential weapons if we sit down to eat at a restaurant or go to the movies. Knowing where to go without having to look for it in the heat of the moment will save time that could be spent acting. After this incident, I'm adding the search for places we could take cover in an emergency.

- **Understand the difference between cover versus concealment.** Every NRA course I've ever taken discusses the difference between cover and concealment. In many cases when you are forced to use your own firearm, there's another person who is ready and willing to shoot back. Concealment is enough to hide you but not enough to protect you from bullets. Cover is something sturdy enough to stop a bullet; a concrete structure like a road divider, the engine block of a car, a refrigerator, a steel door, or a brick wall. When watching the video playback of the Las Vegas shooting, many people were seeking concealment behind flimsy barriers, and that is not enough to protect yourself in a situation with a high-powered gun and a shooter spraying an area.

- **Separate from the crowd.** In a situation like this one, the shooter was trying to take down as many people as possible, so it was most likely he was aiming at the crowd instead of picking off people who moved away from the bulk of the group. One possible strategy would be to get away from the crowd. You and the person/people you are with would be less alluring than a group of a hundred panicked people, all huddled together where maximum harm could be achieved.

- **Don't get down or play dead.** Lots of people crouched down and got as low as they could. In many situations, this would be the best bet, but not this one. The person was shooting from up high, aiming downward. Being still and crouching down wouldn't do much to protect you from a person firing from this angle, nor would playing dead. Action is almost always a better choice than inaction. As well, getting down would make it more likely that you'd be trampled by a panicked crowd of people trying to get away. Clark County Fire Chief Greg Cassell said that some of a "wide range" of injuries included people who were trampled by the panicked crowds.

- **Listen for reload.** In a situation like this, there will be pauses in the shooting when the person stops to either reload or change firearms. That is your opportunity to make a dash for the exits. Don't wait too long to make your move, because it only takes an experienced gunman a few seconds to reload a familiar gun and then your chance is gone.

I'm not an expert. I don't have law enforcement or military experience, so, I spoke to someone far more experienced in this type of thing than I am. Scott Kelley is a former Counterintelligence Special Agent, US Army Chief Warrant Officer and combat veteran, as well as the author of *Graywolf Survival*,[2] and was kind enough to answer all my questions.

TEACHING YOUR KIDS HOW TO SURVIVE A SCHOOL SHOOTING

Imagine getting a phone call like this from your high schooler:

"Mom, there's been a shooting. I'm running."

Those were the chilling words heard by a mother in Kentucky, when her son was fleeing from a classmate who killed two students and injured seventeen more in January 2018. The two fifteen-year-olds died at the hands of another fifteen-year-old boy, who was later arrested.

---

2 http://graywolfsurvival.com/.

Shocked students described the terrifying moment the shooter opened fire before classes began, forcing nearly one hundred children to run out of the school to seek safety.[3]

"He was determined. He knew what he was doing," a classmate said of the shooter.

"It was one right after another, bang-bang-bang-bang-bang. You could see his arm jerking as he was pulling the trigger."

Another student said "No one screamed. It was almost completely silent as people just ran."

"He just ran out of ammo and couldn't do anything else. He took off running and tried to get away from the officers."

. . . Mitchell Garland, who rushed outside his business when he heard about the shooting, described seeing the students flee the school.

"They was running and crying and screaming," he said. "They was just kids running down the highway. They were trying to get out of there."

The scene was utter pandemonium.

It can happen anywhere.

No place is safe from violence these days. This was the tiny town of Benton, Kentucky, population 4,531. In February 2018, seventeen people were killed in a deadly school shooting in Parkland, Florida. The terror is the same, children fleeing or hiding helplessly from someone with superior force.

Would your child know what to do in the event of a school shooting?

There are a few important things to note about school shootings. First, many who are injured are not shot, they get hurt fleeing the

---

3 http://www.dailymail.co.uk/news/article-5305879/Survivors-reveal
-terrifying-moment-15-year-old-opened-fire.html.

scene. Second, first responders often shut down all the exits, meaning the school shooter, and kids who are still inside, can't escape.

Remember, acceptance is the first step to surviving an attack.

This is just the same as it is for adults, but younger people can be even less likely to be prepared to accept a horrifying reality. In many of the descriptions of school shootings, students said they heard a "popping" noise and didn't really grasp what was happening.

As horrific as it is to think through a scenario like this, doing so could save your child's life. This information isn't just for kids in the school system. Even homeschooled kids can find themselves in a situation where they are without a parent and something terrible happens, like sports practice, church events, or other outings.

THE FOUR COURSES OF ACTION

We can't always predict when an attack is about to happen. There might be no indication in your immediate surroundings to alert you to the fact that something is going down. At school, your kids are in comfortable surroundings and they don't have their guards up. They may be blithely unaware until the moment the first shot is fired.

If your child suddenly finds himself/herself in the midst of a school shooting, they need to be ready to take one of the following courses of action:

1. **Escape.** Get as far away from the threat as possible. If you can do so safely, run for the doors, and if you can't get to a door, don't be afraid to pick up a chair and smash out a window. This will take some forethought because most kids would need to get past the mental taboo of destroying school property. Teach kids to run in a zig-zag pattern from cover to cover in order to be more difficult targets.

2. **Take cover.** If you can't get away, get behind something solid and wait for your opportunity to either escape or fight

back. Make sure your kids know the difference between cover and concealment. Many schools have thick concrete walls that will provide sturdy cover, but a wooden door or a desk will not.

3. **Hide.** If you are in another part of the building and you hear shots, your first choice should be to escape. If you aren't in a place where you can safely do that, you may be able to quietly hide somewhere. Bathrooms aren't ideal but hiding quietly in a locked classroom with the lights out may keep you away from the shooter.

4. **Fight back.** This is absolutely a last resort. When you aren't armed, you will be at a serious disadvantage against an armed opponent. The only possible advantage is the element of surprise. Most people with a gun don't expect a direct challenge. If you have no other option whatsoever, you should be prepared to fight for your life. Go in low to knock the shooter down, from behind if possible. A group of students will have a better chance of subduing the shooter than one student alone. Obviously, this is an action to be taken by older kids. Younger children would be unlikely to launch an effective attack.

Some security companies[4] are now doing training with schools to help them respond more effectively in the event of a school shooting. As a parent, encourage your local school board to consider investing in such training.

---

4   http://www.businessinsider.com/teachers-students-alice-fight-defend
-school-mass-shooters.

Chapter 10
HOW TO SURVIVE CIVIL UNREST

The idea of civil unrest isn't a far-fetched notion anymore. We've seen it too often right here in our own country in the past few decades to think that it can't happen here. Think back to the riots in Ferguson, Missouri; Baltimore, Maryland; and across the country in the aftermath of the 2016 presidential election, and you'll realize that any neighborhood could be at risk.

Most of the triggers are situations that we, as individuals, have little control over. Whether it starts with an unpopular judicial verdict, the institution of martial law, a win or loss at a sporting event, or a protest against the police, the cause won't matter if you find yourself swept up in the middle of it or watching from the sidelines. What we *can* control is our response to a crisis. Having a prepared mindset, a defense plan, and a well-stocked home can help keep you and your family out of harm's way. By planning ahead, we can avoid the fear, panic, and confusion and stay away from the rioters who will use any excuse to steal, and the hungry people who are determined to feed their kids no matter who stands in their way.

There's a distinct pattern when society breaks down, and as our society becomes more desperate, poverty-stricken, and lacking of a moral compass, this trend will become more obvious. Note that the "lacking of a moral compass" part doesn't just refer to the rioters and looters, but also to the cops who think that their badges give them permission to behave inappropriately, too:

- An outrage occurs.
- Good people react and protest the outrage.
- Those perpetrating the outrage try to quell the protest because they don't think that the outrage was actually outrageous. (And whether it was or not can fluctuate—in some cases, force is necessitated, but in more and more cases, it is flagrantly gratuitous.)
- Others react to the quelling and join the protest.
- A mob mentality erupts. Thugs say, "Hey, it's a free for all. I'm gonna get some Doritos and while I'm at it, beat the crap out of some folks for fun."
- All hell breaks loose.
- The military gets called in.
- The city burns, and neighborhoods get destroyed, and no one in the area is safe.
- Cops act preemptively, out of fear, and for a time, there is no rule of law.

If you happen to be stuck there, know this: **you're completely on your own.**

Here are the most vital things that you can do in the case of civil unrest:

GET HOME

In a perfect world, we'd all be home, watching the chaos erupt on TV from the safety of our living rooms. However, reality says that some of us will be at work, at school, or in the car when unrest occurs. You need to develop a "get home" plan for all the members of your family, based on the most likely places that they will be.

- **Devise an efficient route for picking up the kids from school.** Be sure that anyone who might be picking up the children already has permission to do so in the school office.

- **Discuss the plan with older kids.** If children could be moved by their schools to a secondary location in the event of a crisis, some families have formulated plans for their older kids to leave the school grounds in such an instance and take a designated route home or to another meeting place.
- **Keep a get-home bag in the trunk** of your car in case you have to set out on foot.
- **Stash some supplies in the bottom of your child's backpack** such as water, snacks, any tools that might be useful, and a map. Be sure your children understand the importance of OPSEC.
- **Find multiple routes home.** Map out alternative back-road ways to get home as well as directions if you must go home on foot.
- **Find hiding places along the way.** If you work or go to school a substantial distance from your home, figure out some places to lay low now, before a crisis situation. Sometimes staying out of sight is the best way to stay safe.
- **Avoid groups of people.** It seems that the mob mentality strikes when large groups of people get together. Folks who would never ordinarily riot in the streets can get swept up by the mass of people who are doing so.

AVOID LAW ENFORCEMENT

Keep in mind that in many civil disorder situations the authorities are to be avoided every bit as diligently as the angry mobs of looters. This isn't me saying that I don't like cops. It's just common sense. While many of the officers involved most likely just want to resolve the situation and go home to their families, the methods being used are not going to be methods most of us wish to encounter.

In a highly charged situation like this, police and military are trained to use the most efficient methods to speedily shut down a conflict. These methods can include tear gas, sound cannons, and outright physical assaults on citizens. It's important to note that fear can be a powerful motivator when deciding how much force is appropriate when addressing a threat. Cops are just as subject to fear as the rest of us. Twenty cops with shields and batons would be quite reasonable to fear an angry mob of hundreds of shouting people.

Your safety when interacting with officials during a martial law situation does not rely on the intentions of police officers and military. It really doesn't matter whether they are trying to crush your rights under what you consider to be a jack-booted heel, or if they are trying to benevolently keep people safe and reestablish peace and harmony.

Here are some suggestions to help keep you safe when dealing with cops and soldiers:

- **Avoid crowds.** If you are in the midst of a crowd, you'll be considered part of the crowd and treated exactly like everyone else in that group. If they get tear-gassed, so will you. It's guilt by association. If the crowd is violent, and you are part of the crowd, you will also be considered violent, and you'll be dealt with accordingly. Legally, you are actually guilty if you are part of a group that is violent.

- **Be polite.** If you have to interact with officers, be courteous. You won't restore the Constitution by arguing with them or threatening them. It's fine to assert your right, you don't have to allow them to search your house without cause, for example, but do so civilly. Belligerence will get you nothing but a beat-down.

- **You don't get to explain.** In a volatile situation, the cops probably aren't going to listen to you when you try to explain that you're just taking that baseball bat in your hand over to your nephew's house, so he can hit some balls in the backyard. No matter how innocent your intentions are, if you're walking like a duck, you're going to be treated like a duck. Training will kick in, and perceived threats will be immediately neutralized by whatever means the cops find necessary.

Underneath the uniform, cops are human. I'm not justifying the brutality, the methods they use, or the assaults on journalists. Cops are just as likely to be swept up in a mob mentality as thugs are during a high stress situation. By understanding this, you can be better prepared.

STAY HOME

Once you make your way home or to your bug-out location, *stay there!*

By staying home, you are minimizing your risk of being caught in the midst of an angry mob or of sitting in stalled traffic while looters run amok. In most scenarios you will be far safer at home than you will be in any type of shelter or refuge situation. (Obviously if there is some type of chemical or natural threat in your immediate neighborhood such as a toxic leak, flood, or forest fire, the whole situation changes; you must use common sense before hunkering down.)

This is when your preparedness supplies will really pay off. If you are ready for minor medical emergencies and illnesses, a grid-down scenario, and a no-comms situation, you will be able to stay safely at home with your family and ride out the crisis in moderate comfort.

Be sure you have, at the minimum, a supply of the following:

- Water
- Prescription medications
- Food
- First aid supplies
- Over-the-counter medications and/or herbal remedies to treat illnesses at home
- A way to get updates about the outside world

TRY TO KEEP YOUR HOME FROM BEING A TARGET

Sometimes, despite our best intentions, the fight comes to us. Defense is two-fold. Your best defense is avoiding the fight altogether. You want to stay under the radar and not draw attention to yourself. The extent to which you strive to do this should be based on the severity of the unrest in your area. Some of the following recommendations are not necessary in an everyday grid-down scenario, but could save your life in a more extreme civil unrest scenario.

- **Keep all the doors and windows locked.** Secure sliding doors with a metal bar. Consider installing decorative gridwork over a door with a large window so that it becomes difficult for someone to smash the glass and reach in to unlock the door.
- **Put dark plastic over the windows.** (Heavy duty garbage bags work well.) If it's safe to do so, go outside and check to see if any light escapes from the windows. If your home is the only one on the block that is well-lit, it becomes a beacon to others.
- **Don't answer the door.** Many home invasions start with an innocent-seeming knock at the door to gain access to your house.
- **Keep pets indoors.** Sometimes criminals use an animal in distress to get a homeowner to open the door for them. Sometimes people are just mean and hurt animals for fun. Either way, it's safer for your furry friends to be inside with you.
- **Keep cooking smells to a minimum.** If everyone else in the neighborhood is hungry, the meat on your grill will draw people like moths to a flame.
- **Remember that first responders may be tied up.** If the disorder is widespread, don't depend on a call to 911 to save you. You must be prepared to save yourself. Also keep in mind, as mentioned earlier, that the cops are not always your friends in these situations.

If, despite your best efforts, your property draws the attention of people with ill intent, you must be ready to defend your family. The only person you can rely on to protect your family is yourself. Here are some scenarios that you may need to face if things escalate.

Fire

Fire is of enormous concern in these types of scenarios. Fire is a cowardly attack that doesn't require any interaction on the part of the arsonist. It flushes out the family inside, leaving you vulnerable to physical assaults.

To be ready for the potential of fire:

- Have fire extinguishers mounted throughout your home. You can buy them in six packs from Amazon. Be sure to test them frequently and maintain them properly.
- Have fire escape ladders that can be attached to a window-sill in all upper story rooms. Drill with them so that your kids know how to use them if necessary.
- Have bug-out bags prepared that contain all of your important documents in case you have to grab and go.

For some, vandalizing and destroying property is the order of the day. Civil unrest can give people of a certain mentality the excuse they need to seek vengeance against those who have more than they do. Tensions can erupt between the "haves" and the "have-nots." When this occurs, destruction of property often is the way these people choose to show their "power."

While this starts out as purely a property crime, the situation can quickly turn violent. If someone is outside bashing the headlights of your vehicle, it isn't a far stretch to think that they will take it a step further if confronted. How to respond to this is a very individual decision and depends to a great extent on your personal skill levels and confidence. For example, I'm a single mom with daughters. As much as I like my Jeep, it's unlikely that I'd confront an angry mob destroying it, because that just wouldn't be sensible. Things can be replaced, but you and your family members cannot.

If you are a person who is unaccustomed to physical confrontations, you may be better off staying inside and calling your insurance company after the fact. No possession is worth your life or the lives of your family.

Defending Your Home

Some people are adamant that firearms are unnecessary at best and evil at worst. If that is your opinion, you may want to skip over this next section.

In some situations, you may have to defend your home. And for this, *you must be armed.* Chances are, you won't have to unholster your weapon. But this is a plan based on pure luck, and survival favors the prepared. I do not base my preparations for my family on the hope for good luck.

Firearms are an equalizer. A small woman can defend herself from multiple large intruders with a firearm, if she's had some training and knows how to use it properly. Put a kitchen knife in her hand against those same intruders, and her odds decrease exponentially. If you find yourself in a situation in which the lives of you and your loved ones are in danger, there is no substitute for meeting force with force. You may not wish to engage, but sometimes there's no time to escape. Sometimes there's no place to escape to. In these situations, you won't be able to talk your way out of it, hide from it, or throw dishes at the intruders to fight them off.

- **Don't rely on 911.** If the disorder is widespread, don't depend on a call to 911 to save you—you must be prepared to save yourself. First responders may be tied up, and in some cases, the cops may not be on your side. In the aftermath of Hurricane Katrina, some officers joined in the crime sprees, and others stomped all over the 2nd Amendment and confiscated people's legal firearms at a time when they needed them most.

- **Be armed and keep your firearm on your person.** When the door of your home is breached, you can be pretty sure the people coming in are not there to make friendly conversation over a nice cup of tea. Make a plan to greet them with a deterring amount of force. Be sure to keep your firearm on your person during this type of situation, because there won't be time to go get it from your gun safe. Don't even go to the kitchen to get a snack without it. Home invasions go down in seconds, and you have to be constantly ready.

- **Know how to use your firearm.** Whatever your choice of weapon, practice, practice, practice. A weapon you don't know how to use is more dangerous than having no weapon at all.

- **Make sure your children are familiar with the rules of gun safety.** Of course, it should go without saying that you will have preemptively taught your children the rules of gun safety so that no horrifying accidents occur. In fact, it's my fervent hope that any child old enough to do so has been taught to safely and effectively use a firearm themselves. Knowledge is safety.

- **Have a safe room established for children or other vulnerable family members.** If the worst happens and your home is breached, you need to have a room that family members can escape to.[1] I'm not talking about a Jodie Foster *Panic Room*, but something you can DIY to harden an existing part of your home. This room needs to have a heavy exterior door instead of a regular hollow core interior door. There should be communication devices in the room so that the person can call for help, as well as a reliable weapon to be used in the unlikely event that the safe room is breached. The family members should be instructed not to come out of

---

1   https://www.theorganicprepper.com/how-to-create-a-safe-room -in-your-house-or-apartment.

that room **FOR ANY REASON** until you give them the all clear or help has arrived.

- **Plan an escape route.** If the odds are against you, devise a way to get your family to safety. Your property is not worth your life. Be wise enough to know if you're getting into a fight that you can't win.

So many times, when interviewed after a disaster, people talk about being shocked at the behavior of others. Their level of cognitive dissonance has lulled them into thinking that we're safe and that we live in a civilized country. They are unwilling to accept that civilization is only a glossy veneer, even when the evidence of that is right in front of them, aiming a gun at their faces, lighting their homes on fire, or brutalizing their loved ones.

They refuse to arm themselves and prepare for an uncivilized future.

Accept it now, make a plan, and you'll be ready to take action when all hell breaks loose.

CIVIL UNREST CHECKLIST

Every civil unrest scenario is different. You must make a personal plan based on your environment, your neighbors, and the type of situation that triggered the unrest. By thinking ahead, you've already increased your family's chances at surviving unscathed.

- Check your pantry and fill any gaps in your food preps.
- Get cash in small denominations out of the bank.
- Make sure you have enough garbage bags, pet supplies, and toiletries.
- Make sure all electronics are fully charged and keep them charged during the lead-up to an event.
- Make sure any cell phone battery packs are fully charged.
- Fill your gas tank up to the max.

- If your vehicle isn't in a garage, park it trunk-end in, as close to a wall as you can. This makes it harder to get to the tank to either steal the fuel or set fire to it.
- Check your home security; walk around looking at your property as if you were a burglar, and take appropriate action to improve security if required.
- Have something on hand for the kids to do in case of school closures.
- Make sure you have a fully stocked first aid kit, prescription medications, and OTC medications.
- Check and clean your firearms.
- Pick up some extra ammo.
- Plan to keep pets indoors.

Resources:

Chapter 11

HOW TO SURVIVE PERSONAL FINANCIAL PROBLEMS

Personal financial problems can happen for a variety of reasons, and not all of them are your fault. You may have a large medical bill, the need for a vital home repair, the loss of a stream of income, or the death of a breadwinner. More importantly, even if your financial problems came directly from a string of bad decisions, it's essential to stop beating yourself up and tackle the problem.

How can you prep for financial problems?
Preppers think about a lot of doomy, gloomy stuff regarding various types of apocalypses. After all, disaster is everywhere. However, there is *one* major disaster that is the most likely to befall any of us at some point in our lives and it isn't zombies, North Koreans, or the plague.

It's financial problems.

You may be currently having this issue right now. Maybe you don't make enough money. Maybe the primary breadwinner has lost his or her job. Maybe someone has massive medical expenses. Maybe there is some other epic expense that you never saw coming. It doesn't matter how it happens, it just matters that you see it as something for which you need to prepare. Financial stability is one of the most important preparations you can make.

THE 3 KEYS TO SURVIVING FINANCIAL PROBLEMS

Financial stability doesn't come from being wealthy. In fact, you can make a million dollars in a year but if you spend a million and one dollars, you aren't really financially stable. Instead, financial stability comes from being able to dial back your spending if necessary, and deal with a monetary emergency. It comes from being able to pay your bills and have some money left over. It comes from being prepared for that rainy day that we all hope will never happen.

While having more money definitely helps with this, having more money isn't always possible. You can work around this, though; in most cases it is far easier to spend less than it is to make more. Frugality can completely change your life.

If you focus on the three steps below, you can turn your financial situation around.

1. Reduce Your Monthly Expenses

We can justify all sorts of frivolous expenditures. Most people are great at saying why they *have* to live in a super-expensive home or why every member of the family *must* have a cell phone or why they *deserve* an exorbitant recurring expense, but they aren't very good at cutting those expenses.

The most valuable thing you can do while trying to get your financial feet on the ground is to drop your expenses to rock bottom. Maybe . . .

- the kids could share a room.
- you could drop to one car.
- you could set a grocery budget instead of buying whatever looks tasty at the time.
- you could take a walk instead of going to a gym.

There are a ton of ways to lower your monthly living expenses. Some of them are a bit more radical and others are not quite as extreme.

The lower your expenses are, the less money *you have* to make. This is extremely important because as I mentioned before, it is far easier to control the money you are spending than the money you are making.

2. Stock up When Times Are Good

When times are good, people tend to purchase extravagant things that they normally wouldn't spend money on, like an outrageously expensive outfit, a pricey vehicle, or an exotic vacation. I agree it's very important to reward yourself sometimes. Life shouldn't always be grim and desperate. At the same time, you need to be practical, too, because if one thing is true about money, it's that there are good times and bad ones. When the money is rolling in and the expenses are low, stock up on things that you normally need to buy, such as:

- Food for the freezer and pantry.
- Paper towels and toilet paper.
- Personal hygiene products.
- School supplies for the kids.
- First aid supplies.

Then, during a downturn in your finances, you don't need to use your limited funds to pay for these necessities.

Once, when I was laid off, I went for five months without being able to find another job. The small amount that I received from unemployment insurance was able to keep a roof over our heads, a car in the driveway, and the utilities on. For those months, I hardly had to buy anything for our day-to-day needs because I had a pantry simply loaded with those supplies that had been purchased during better times. As a single parent and the only breadwinner, my pantry was the only reason we didn't end up homeless.

3. Build an Emergency Fund

Hand in hand with stocking up is putting some money back. A recent survey[1] showed that 63 percent of Americans don't have enough money to see them through a $1,000 emergency. Is this you? If it is, you need to change it, because you are literally *one missed paycheck* away from disaster.

Think about how easy it is to miss a paycheck. What if you are too sick to work? What if a client fails to pay you? What if the business you are working for suddenly closes its doors?

You should do everything you can to put back at least one month's worth of expenses—preferably three to six months:

- Sell something.
- Get a second job.
- Put money back each time you are paid.

This is money that is not to be touched except for a true emergency, like the car breaking down, an illness, or a job loss. It isn't for going to a concert you got invited to at the last minute, funding a vacation, or buying a new outfit. Trust me, if you need it, it will be an incredible relief to have it. I can tell you this from multiple experiences.

If you aren't making a whole lot of money right now, saving just $10 a week can really add up, it's more than $500 over the course of a year. If you're anything like the rest of the world, you probably blow $10 a week on fancy coffee, magazines, or some other frivolous expense, right? Being financially stable is more about your mindset than your income. People with lower incomes can do astounding things with some focus and dedication.

Remember, no one is immune to financial problems.

---

1   https://www.theorganicprepper.com/without-an-emergency-fund
-you-are-one-missed-paycheck-from-disaster.

EIGHT STEPS TO SURVIVING A JOB LOSS

A 2014 report on jobs[2] showed some alarming statistics: one in five Americans have lost their jobs over the past five years and remained unemployed. When the US economy suffers, the lower and middle classes are usually the people taking the hit, and unless you live in a neighborhood of rainbows and unicorns, it's a good bet that this has happened to either your family or someone you know. Sometimes the layoff is expected, as you see your company's profits dwindling. Other times, it is completely out of the blue when you get called into the manager's office and handed your walking papers. Either way, when the axe falls, you may feel as though you're reeling in shock. Well, tough love, here: Get a hold of yourself! The first steps you take can help you to survive until you get a new source of income.

This chapter is not about how to prep for a personal financial collapse. (That's coming up next.) It's about those essential first moves once the job is gone.

In the intro to this book, I wrote about the three steps for surviving any disaster, and job loss is no exception. You must *accept* that the event has occurred, you must make a *plan*, and you must *act* on that plan.

Aside from that, here's what you need to do right away to minimize the damage to your personal finances when a sudden job loss occurs:

1. Don't sign anything right away.

As much loyalty as you may have had to your company, they clearly don't feel the same sense of loyalty towards you. Many companies will try to get you to sign paperwork right away to "settle the details." Trust me when I say these details will be skewed in their favor and not yours. You *do not* have to sign anything while sitting there stunned at your sudden change in circumstances.

---

2   http://news.rutgers.edu/research-news/long-term-unemployed-struggle
-economy-improves-rutgers-study-finds/20140925#.VTUBUCHBzGd.

It's vital that you take the time to read over everything carefully. Your severance package, your 401K, any accrued pension, and unemployment benefits will be at risk. In some cases, you can negotiate this, even though you are not sitting in the power seat.

Don't commit to any type of agreement while you're reeling, *particularly* if they try to coerce you into signing immediately. Regardless of what you may be told, any delay in your unemployment benefits or severance will be minimal.

2. Begin a total spending freeze for a couple of days.

One of the biggest mistakes people make when faced with a shocking job loss is to go on spending as though they still have an income. Perhaps they go and buy something to try and make themselves feel better. Maybe they just continue spending like they always did, with hundreds of dollars going out for kids' activities, dinners out, and shopping trips.

Just. Stop.

You need a few days to reassess your budget and see where you're at. You don't want to regret the expenditures you make right after a job loss. Put yourself on a complete spending freeze for the next few days while you assess the change in your financial situation.

3. Apply for unemployment benefits.

Unemployment is not welfare. It is something that you paid into the entire time you were employed. Please don't feel guilty about taking the money that is rightfully yours. Keep in mind that it can take up to two months for your benefits to start, and that any money from your severance package can delay the onset of benefits.

Unemployment is only a portion of what you made when you were employed, so a revamp of the budget is still a must. Send in your application immediately so that you know where you stand and when you can expect the money to start coming in.

4. Create a budget for necessities.

It's absolutely vital that you drop your expenditures to the bare minimum until you are able to get another stream of income. You need to take a look at where your money goes and base your new budget on the necessities. Although having a vehicle in each stall of the garage and an iPhone in the hand of every family member is nice, these are not necessary to sustaining life.

What are actual necessities?

- Water
- Food (and the ability to cook it)
- Medicine and medical supplies
- Basic hygiene supplies
- Shelter (including sanitation, lights, heat)
- Simple tools
- Seeds
- Defense items

Absolutely everything beyond those basic necessities is a luxury.

So, by this definition, what luxuries do you have?

5. Slash luxury spending.

Reduce your monthly payments by cutting frivolous expenses. Look at every single monthly payment that comes out of your bank account and slash relentlessly. Consider cutting the following, at least temporarily:

- Cable
- Cell phones
- Home phones
- Gym memberships
- Restaurant meals
- Unnecessary driving

- Entertainment such as trips to the movies, the skating rink, or the mall

You don't have to cut these things out forever, but until you reach some financial equilibrium, you need to be as frugal as possible.

6. Start looking for new streams of income.

You know those people who tell you that it's easy to find a new job if you wouldn't be such a snob?

Ignore them.

The job market of today is not the job market of a decade ago. Jobs are few and far between, and good jobs are as elusive as unicorns in Central Park. You may need to look at creating your own streams of income. Here are a few ideas:

- Create an online business
- Use your expertise from your former job to work as a consultant
- Do various small jobs
- Create a home-based business with a low start-up cost (Now's not the time to make a large investment)
- Use creative skills to make things to sell
- Provide a service (Maybe you can cook, sew, repair things, or build things. Lots of people can't and are willing to pay someone who can)

You want a project that doesn't require a lot of inventory and supplies, a market to which you can sell, and a way to get the word out at little or no cost.

7. Sell stuff.

All that stuff you've been meaning to go through in the basement just might be the key to keeping a roof over your head. It's time to start an eBay account, have a yard sale, or get on Craigslist and start selling things that have just been sitting there for a while.

Your trash might be another person's treasure. Instead of regifting those things in your attic, sell them so they can become someone else's clutter. You'd be surprised how much money you can make while decluttering your home.

8. Look for the silver lining.

Although job loss can be terrifying, it can also be the start of something wonderful.

When I lost my job in the automotive industry, I was devastated. As a single mom, how was I going to continue taking care of my two girls with no income? Instead of being a bad thing, it turned out to be the best thing that ever happened to me. I was able to take the writing I'd been dabbling in for years from a hobby to a full-time job. I made a conscious decision *not* to search for another job, but to follow my dream of being a writer and editor. Maybe I succeeded because it was do-or-die time. There was no option but to make it work. I began writing for other websites, started my own site, and began outlining books.

As it turned out, that shocking, unceremonious discussion in the manager's office was a turning point in my life. I've read many success stories that began the same way. Maybe yours will, too! Sometimes what seems like an ending can actually be a new beginning.

DEALING WITH DEBT

Many Americans owe so much money that they have no idea how they'll manage to pay it off, with the holiday season making it that much worse. Even though the bills haven't come rolling in yet, a 2016 survey[3] from T. Rowe Price speculated that average spending is $422 per child. (Which means half of Americans intended to spend more than that.) Because many Americans have little cash to spare, it's a safe bet that these Christmas gifts were directly added to credit card debt.

---

3   http://moneyconfidentkids.com/content/money-confident-kids/en/us
    /media/news/more-than-half-of-parents-try-to-get-everything-on-kids
    -holiday-wish-lists-no-matter-the-cost.html.

Debt that is already astronomical, by the way. Household debt is over $12 trillion and climbing. Blogger Michael Snyder broke it down into numbers[4] that are easier to grasp:

> *It breaks down to about $38,557 for every man, woman, and child in the entire country. So, if you have a family of four, your share comes to a grand total of $154,231, and that doesn't even include corporate debt, local government debt, state government debt, or the gigantic debt of the federal government. That number is only for household debt, and there aren't too many Americans that could cough up their share right at this moment.*

And to make matters even worse, 35 percent of these indebted Americans owe money that is past due by 180 days or more.

If you're in debt, there is a way to dig your way out. The best book I ever read about paying off debt is *The Total Money Makeover* by Dave Ramsey. You may be able to find it at your local library, but if you can't, I suggest you buy it. Even if you are struggling financially, I recommend scrimping someplace so you can manage to purchase the book if you are trying to pay off debt and get back on your feet.

Dave recommends something called "The Snowball Method" for repaying debt quickly. Imagine a snowball at the top of a hill. As you roll the snowball, you pick up more snow, and the snowball gets bigger. By the time it's at the bottom of the hill, it's huge. You can do the same thing with debt by paying off the smallest bill first, then applying what you'd normally pay on that lowest bill to the next bill. Continue adding the minimum payment for each paid-off bill to the next largest one until all of your debt is repaid.

This method assumes you have enough money coming in to make your basic payments, plus a little bit extra. I have personally used this technique to attack debt, with a few tweaks of my own.

---

4   http://theeconomiccollapseblog.com/archives/america-the-debt-pig-we -are-a-buy-now-pay-later-society-and-pay-later-is-rapidly-approaching.

Here's a more detailed explanation of how the Snowball Method works.

1. Write down every penny you owe. This is tough love, and it's painful (okay—excruciating) but go through all your bills and write down your totals. Most people find that the total is higher than they expected. The good news is, if you are truly committed to paying off your debt, this is the highest that it will be.

2. Organize the bills from smallest to largest amounts. This may not seem like it makes much sense, but trust me . . . there's a method to the madness here. If you have two debts of the same amount, prioritize the one with the highest interest rate.

3. Write another list of the minimum payments for each bill. This is your baseline of payments each month. For this exercise, let's say there are ten bills with a total of $750 in monthly minimum payments.

4. Now, figure out the rest of your budget. (We'll go into this in more detail in the next section.) Once you pay your rent/mortgage, buy groceries, and pay the utility bills, how much money do you have on top of your $750 a month? For this exercise, we'll say you have an extra $100.

5. Your worksheet might look something like this:

CARD	BALANCE	MINIMUM PAYMENT
VICTORIA'S SECRET	$100	$20
JCPENNEY'S	$150	$25
TARGET	$350	$40
KOHL'S	$400	$45
AMAZON	$1000	$70
SEARS	$1100	$75
HOME DEPOT	$1700	$105
VISA	$2200	$120
MASTER CARD	$2300	$125
LINE OF CREDIT	$3500	$125
TOTALS	$12800	$750

6. Now, you're going to start putting all of your extra money toward the lowest bill each month. So, the first month, you make all of your minimum payments, put $80 extra on the Victoria's Secret bill to pay it off, and then apply your leftover $20 to the JCPenney's bill.

Card	Balance	Minimum Payment
~~Victoria's Secret~~	~~$100~~	~~$20~~ $20+80
JCPenney's	$150	$25 +$20
Target	$350	$40
Kohl's	$400	$45
Amazon	$1000	$70
Sears	$1100	$75
Home Depot	$1700	$105
Visa	$2200	$120
Master Card	$2300	$125
Line of Credit	$3500	$125
Totals	$12800	$750

7. The following month, take the minimum payment from Victoria's Secret, the minimum from JCPenney's, and your extra $100 to pay off your JCPenney's debt. Keep in mind that due to interest, your other debts will not change much at all if you are only making the minimum payment. For the sake of this exercise, we're leaving them as they are to demonstrate that.

Card	Balance	Minimum Payment
~~Victoria's Secret~~	~~$100~~	~~$20~~
~~JCPenney's~~	~~$150~~	~~$25~~ +$20 +$100
Target	$350	$40
Kohl's	$400	$45
Amazon	$1000	$70
Sears	$1100	$75
Home Depot	$1700	$105
Visa	$2200	$120
Master Card	$2300	$125
Line of Credit	$3500	$125
Totals	$12800	$750

8. The month after that, you'll combine all of your previous minimum payments with your extra $100, plus the minimum for Target for a total of $185 against that bill. It will take you two months of snowballing to pay this off.

CARD	BALANCE	MINIMUM PAYMENT
~~VICTORIA'S SECRET~~	~~$100~~	~~$20~~
~~JCPENNEY'S~~	~~$150~~	~~$25~~
TARGET	$350	~~$40~~ $40 + $25 + $20 + $100
KOHL'S	$400	$45
AMAZON	$1000	$70
SEARS	$1100	$75
HOME DEPOT	$1700	$105
VISA	$2200	$120
MASTER CARD	$2300	$125
LINE OF CREDIT	$3500	$125
TOTALS	$12800	$750

And that's how you pay off consumer debt quickly.

Do you get the idea? Instead of flailing away with minimum payments and a little extra when you can, make a concrete plan to take down debt as fast as possible. It can feel strange to only make minimum payments on the larger debts, but trust me, this is much more efficient than just paying a little extra here and there. If you get new windfalls while you're paying off debt, like tax returns or bonuses, apply them to your smallest bills.

Sometimes we get into debt due to bad decisions and sometimes it's out of desperation. If you have ever been without money for groceries or utilities, you may have used a credit card even though you knew it wasn't a good idea. Maybe you had a great income when you incurred the debt but then lost your job. There are many reasons you could find yourself way over your head. That's all in the past. Don't beat yourself up, because that's ultimately counterproductive. Just commit to getting out of debt as quickly as you can and do your best to avoid the same pitfall in the future.

HOW TO CREATE (AND STICK TO) A BUDGET

Lots of experts will give you excellent advice on how to create a budget. Creating a budget is actually pretty easy. You figure out what your expenses are, take this from your income, and then figure out what to do with the money you have left over.

Sticking to the budget . . . that's the tough part. This is where most people experience financial failure. They know what they should be doing, but that little treat is just calling out to them, and they think *one off-plan expense won't matter.* Or perhaps they have a spouse who is not really on board with the whole budget business and they are constantly playing catch-up because of unplanned expenses. The economy is certainly not getting any better, so it's important to get control of your finances *now.* With careful planning, you can keep everyone happy, have the occasional treat, and still stick to your budget.

Budgeting is like dieting.

Really, if you think about it, a budget is a lot like a diet. Everyone hates doing it, but sometimes our pants won't zip, and we've got to do something about it. So, you figure out what your caloric intake should be. Every bite of food you eat should be measured and accounted for and you subtract the amounts from your allotted intake. Sometimes you have an off-plan meal: a piece of cake at a birthday party, a celebratory dinner out, or an ice cream cone with the kiddos. You have to account for this, too, and you can't do it too often, or your diet will fail. Sometimes you have loved ones who sabotage your good intentions, either deliberately or thoughtlessly. They might be food pushers (come on, one bite won't kill you), guilters (but I made this especially for you), or influencers (just because I buy chips doesn't mean you have to eat them). Whatever the case, the result can be the same, your careful plan is in shambles.

It's exactly the same with money.

It is often the influence of others, no matter how well-meaning, that causes you to go over you financial "calorie limit." If you plan carefully, you can allow yourself some wiggle room to enjoy something outside of your normal diet (or budget). For example, when dieting, if you know that you have a party to attend, you might eat fewer calories on the day leading up to the event so that you can splurge without guilt. When budgeting, if you know there is an outing planned, you might cut back a bit on the grocery bill that week in order to have extra money to spend during your event.

When dieting, if you want a treat, you can have it, but you might be eating steamed veggies for the rest of the day if that treat is the equivalent of your daily caloric intake. Likewise, with spending, if you want a Disney vacation, you can have it, but you might need to live in your uncle's car, since you won't also be able to afford to pay for that, your mortgage, and your car payment. Eating whatever you want can have unpleasant consequences. So can spending whatever you want.

Here's how to create a budget.

For those of you who have created a budget before, feel free to skip over this part.

Creating a budget is simple. In one column, you have your money in, and in another column, you have your money out.

Money in might be:

- Salary from work
- Bonus check
- Tax return
- Alimony or child support
- Rents due to you from property you own

Money out might be:

- Mortgage/rent
- Utility bills

- Credit card bills
- Car payment
- Insurances
- Loan payments
- Debt payments
- Groceries
- Miscellaneous spending

Your first step is figuring out those two totals. In most cases, your money in will be more than your money out. If it isn't, you have a serious problem and you need to look at lowering your fixed expenses ASAP, or your financial problems will spiral far out of control.

Assuming you have some money left over, this is for your variable expenses. You may want to allot this money to savings, to preps, to paying off debt, or to spending money for the members of your family.

Are you surprised when you see the numbers there in black and white? Maybe you bring in more than you thought. Maybe you are spending more than you realized. Either way, now that you can look at it all on paper, the next part will be a lot easier.

Sticking to the budget.

So, planning the budget is easy. Anyone who can do basic math can create a budget. But how do you stick to it and get your finances under control?

Control . . . that's the key word.

This is the method that I use. Feel free to adapt it to your situation.

I have a bank account that I use specifically for fixed expenses. All of my payments out go through that account. Everything that is not earmarked for bills comes out of the account and is used for discretionary spending. I don't carry a debit card with me for this account, to reduce the temptation of knowing I have that money there.

The money that comes out is immediately organized into . . . mint tins. (Finally, another use for those little tins!) The tins go into the safe until they are needed. It's like the envelope method, but in a different container.

If there is money left over after I've sorted my variable expenses into the mint tins, this goes into my wallet and is my spending money. I keep grocery money in (you guessed it) a mint tin in my purse. When spending grocery money, the change and the receipt go into my tin. That way, I know I'm sticking to my budget for food. When the tin is empty, it means I'm out of grocery money. Sometimes I have extra money left at the end of the week, and that stays in the grocery money tin to allow me to make some large bulk purchases.

Some of the variable expenses that I delegate money to are:

- Emergency fund
- Gasoline
- Groceries/stockpile
- College expenses for my daughters
- Preps
- Medical expenses/dental care
- Vision care
- Clothes
- Spending money
- Gifts (a little each week toward holidays, birthdays, etc.)
- Fun money (for road trips, school field trips, dinner out, and miscellaneous adventures)
- Garden supplies (this is my addiction! Seeds, plants, tools, oh my!)

It's important to prioritize these areas.

Just because there is money in the tin doesn't mean it gets spent each month. The beauty of this is that you less frequently have a big expense that you haven't planned for. If my daughter needs new glasses, the money is there, available for the appointment. If we want to go visit a museum or national park, we have some money set aside to do that.

Alternatively, if the tin is empty, the expense has to wait. Maybe the birthday celebration will be a bit humbler, the greenhouse will have to wait to be purchased for a few more months, or we'll have to make do with clothing that is a little snug for a couple more weeks. Our entertainment will be limited to Netflix, a nature walk, or a trip to the library.

Like I said, the key to this is control. One person has to be in control of the finances. I'm not recommending that anybody become a tyrant, doling out nickels after a family member begs and pleads. However, if anyone can just go and help themselves to the money that has been budgeted, this is not going to work. If you're part of a couple, unless both partners are completely on the same page, the person with the best financial sense needs to hold the key to the safe.

I know that if you've just been shaking your head, paying off the credit card bill, and belly-aching a little each month, that your family isn't going to like this. You'll probably have to listen to some adamant complaints but it will be worth it in the end when you have the peace of mind that comes with having your budget under control.

A budget is not about a total spending freeze.

Most people hear the word budget and automatically cringe, picturing a state of horrible deprivation, old clothes, and perhaps their big toes poking through that hole in their sneakers. Much like the word "diet" (see above) "budget" is thought of in negative terms.

I'm not going to lie, sometimes it's like that, especially if things are really out of control.

But usually, at least after the first couple of months, it isn't bad at all. Being on a budget doesn't mean that you can't spend money. It means that you plan for your expenditures so that you can afford the stuff of everyday life. It means that you pay for the necessities first and that you get the extras second. It means that you scrutinize where your money is going, and you make certain that your purchases are worthwhile. Do you really want that fancy meal out each week, or would you rather put that money toward a fun family outing at the end of the month? It means that those expenses that you know will come up (like new eyeglasses) will be planned for, and they won't make an enormous dent when it's time to pay for them, leaving you rolling pennies for gasoline to get to work.

Embrace frugality.

As a parent, sometimes I've asked my kids to do things they don't want to do. (Haven't we all?) The biggest key to their success in the endeavor is their attitude.

Scenario #1:

Me: "Kiddo, it's time to swap your winter clothes for your spring clothes. Please go through your closet, sort through your winter clothes, and get rid of the stuff that's too small or that you don't want anymore."

Kiddo: "I don't want to! I hate this! It's not fair!!!"

Kiddo goes through the closet, angrily shoving things in a garbage bag without taking a good hard look at things. She sulks, pouts, and is otherwise miserable. She gets the job done but makes sure that it is unpleasant for all of us.

Scenario #2:

Me: "Kiddo, it's time to swap your winter clothes for your spring clothes. Please go through your closet, sort through your winter clothes, and get rid of the stuff that's too small or that you don't want anymore."

Kiddo: "Okay—this gives me a chance to see if there's anything I can repurpose, too!"

Kiddo goes through the closet, eagerly sorting items into piles. She comes up with a good stash of "new" materials for craft projects, a bag of donations, and two shirts that were buried at the back that she forgot she had. The job is done, and the end result is its own reward.

Switching over to a more frugal lifestyle can be just like the above scenarios. You can embrace it and relish the challenge of it, or you can sulk, pout, and be absolutely miserable. Sometimes people feel as though they shouldn't *have* to be frugal. They work hard, and they deserve treats.

However, I *choose* to live frugally. I opt to live a thrifty, non-consumer lifestyle because of my personal experiences. Disengaging from the uncaring financial machine has provided me with a freedom I never had when I was bringing in close to six figures in a corporate game of mousetrap.

THE STORY BEHIND MY ADVENT INTO CHEAPSKATERY

I suffered some great financial losses back in 2010. I lost my house, my car, and my business. We had been living frugally in comparison to many people, but not frugally enough to counteract that personal economic disaster. Looking back, I'm not sure if any amount of frugality could have really made a difference.

It was a devastating blow, and it came right on the heels of the loss of my sweet father. We became even more thrifty out of necessity, and I resented the need to do so every single time I stepped into a mall, purchased groceries, or emptied my bank account on payday to keep the utilities on and a roof over our heads, with nothing extra left over for fun, or even secondary needs. It was a very grim time for our family.

When the depression began to lift, I saw that getting out from under that mountain of debt had actually provided me with a gift of enormous freedom. I realized that my life could take a different turn. I was no longer tied to anything.

And that's when I began to embrace my cheap side.

I realized that I no longer needed to buy into the system that had been the source of my personal economic crisis. By supporting it, I wasn't supporting us. By being as self-sufficient as possible, by cutting my spending, and by not needing "the system," I was winning. I was becoming truly free.

When an entity has nothing to hold over your head, all the options are your own. You can make your decisions based on what is good for you and your family, not on what terrible things might happen to you if you don't "toe the line."

HOW TO EMBRACE YOUR CHEAP SIDE

Hardcore frugality is not just making a choice to buy the generic brand of laundry soap instead of a jug of Tide with scent beads. Hardcore frugality is buying the ingredients to make five times the amount of laundry soap for half the price of that name brand detergent, all the while *loving* the fact that the Proctors and the Gambles are not getting your money.

When you can cross that line between resenting the fact that you have to strictly budget to embracing the fact that by being as frugal as possible, you have a freedom you never dreamed of before, then you have begun to embrace your cheap side.

Being a black belt in frugality takes creativity and an optimistic outlook. It should never be some grim, sad thing that you have to do. It should be something that you choose to do. By finding joy in your non-consumerism, you will be far more successful at it. It becomes a game that you win if you can do something for free that others spend money on.

When you feel like you require less, you in turn become happy with less. This means that the money that you have goes a lot further.

HOW TO BECOME A HAPPY NON-CONSUMER

- **Be grateful.** An "attitude of gratitude" is the most vital part of embracing your cheap side. If you're happy with what you've got, you will find that you "need" far less than you did before. That's because you aren't seeking some momentary hit of joyous adrenaline by purchasing something. That rush rarely lasts and you're just left with more stuff and less money.

- **Be creative.** How can you make something, save something, or repair something in a totally original way? Embrace the challenge and tap into your creativity; you may just discover that, in your originality, you've come up with something far better than the purchased alternative. (We've found this to be especially true with fashion accessories, home decor, and birthday parties!)

- **Give.** Don't let your pursuit of frugality make you stingy. There are always people who are worse off than you. It's important to give a hand up to those people. If your kids were hungry, or cold, or without shelter, wouldn't you hope that some kind person would help them? Even at our absolute rock bottom financially, we donated one can of spaghetti sauce and a package of noodles to the food bank every week, which hopefully provided a warm comforting meal for someone who needed it. It isn't really necessary to debate whether people are truly in need or just milking the system. That is a subject for them and their consciences. Just give. You are responsible for your intentions, not theirs.

- **Spend your money where it really matters.** We opted to move to a very small community into a drafty little cabin in the woods. We made this decision as a family, in order to reduce our monthly output. By getting rid of "city rent" and all of the bills that came with it, we cut our monthly output in half. This means that I can spend a little extra on high-quality meats and dairy, for example. When my daughter needs new glasses, it's not a problem to pay for them. It means my daughters can get through college without crippling student loans.

- **Less need equals more time.** Not only does a thrifty lifestyle mean that I can refocus where my money goes. It means that I can refocus where my time goes. I don't have to work quite as hard on stuff outside the home and can focus on farm and family. I have the time to make hats and scarves instead of purchasing them. I have time to garden and can reap the harvests. I have time to perform money-saving tasks like cooking from scratch, which goes into a big happy circle of having more money to put toward important things.

- **Stay home.** When you stay home more, you are tempted less. You aren't thirsty, requiring a beverage. You aren't hungry, requiring a snack. You aren't using the car, requiring gas. You aren't tempted by all the colorful and wonderful things in the stores.

- **Hang out with like-minded people.** It is so much easier to embrace your cheap side if you don't have people telling you how deprived you are all the time or berating you for being too cheap to spend $27.85 on a movie ticket, popcorn, and a soda pop. Most of my closest friends are thrifty. We swap clothing, we borrow and lend tools, and we cheerfully hang out without spending a dime. Instead of going out to sit in a boutique coffee shop sipping a $6 latte with whipped cream, we sit in the garden at one of our houses sipping a coffee that one of us made, along with a nice fresh blueberry muffin. We enjoy the same conversation we would have had at that coffee shop, too. Instead of heading to the mall, we chat on Skype. When your nearest and dearest are on the same page, life is a whole lot easier.

- **Turn off the TV.** People go to school for years to study how to make people want what they don't need. That great big brainwash box sitting in the living room is a direct pipeline into your brain. From the beautiful homes on the TV programs, the fancy clothes and cars, and the ads for food, recreation, and new cars, the whole racket is designed to make you feel that what you have now is inferior to what you *could* have. Kids are the biggest target of product placement advertising in popular shows. If you watch TV, limit it. Become aware of the scams and discuss them with your kids so that they can easily identify how marketers are attempting to manipulate them. (Confession: we do watch a little bit of TV in our home, and when we do, it's a big game to identify the hidden ads. While this may sound contrary to the advice to turn the TV off, I believe that some limited viewing coupled with an awareness of the marketing techniques inoculates my children against the sales pitch.)

To switch over to a frugal lifestyle successfully, you really have to want to do it. If you're constantly bemoaning what you don't have, you'll be miserable. If you are resentful that you can't have "stuff" then you won't stick to your frugal plan. The most important thing of all is to switch off your personal "want" button. When you don't want or need the things that the big corporations are selling, then you are suddenly free of their restrictions. You are no longer a slave to the wages you must earn to pay for the things they tell you that you should have. You don't have a lifestyle built on expectations, debt, and the never-ending search for happiness bought from a store. (For more fantastically frugal ideas, check out my monthly newsletter, *The Cheapskate's Guide to the Galaxy*.)

WHAT TO DO WHEN YOU SIMPLY CAN'T PAY YOUR BILLS

Unfortunately, sometimes paying off debt, sticking to a budget, and being thrifty aren't enough. You're in a position in which you simply can't pay your bills.

Let's talk about poverty.

I don't mean the kind you're talking about when your friends invite you to go shopping or for a night out and you say, "No, I can't. I'm poor right now." I don't mean the situation when you'd like to get a nicer car but decide you should just stick to the one you have because you don't have a few thousand for a down payment. I don't mean the scene at the grocery store when you decide to get ground beef instead of steak. I'm talking about when you have already done the weird mismatched meals from your pantry that are made up of cooked rice, stale crackers, and a can of peaches, and you've moved on to wondering what on earth you're going to feed your kids. Or when you get an eviction notice for non-payment of rent, a shut-off notice for your utilities, and a repo notice for your car and there's absolutely nothing you can do about any of those notices because there *is no money.*

If you've never been this level of broke, I'm very glad.

I *have* been this broke. I know that it is soul-destroying when no matter how hard you work, how many part-time jobs you squeeze in, and how much you cut, you simply don't make enough money for you and your family to survive in the world today. Being part of the working poor is incredibly frustrating and discouraging.

It is a sickening feeling when you're just barely hanging in there and suddenly, an unexpected expense crops up and decimates your tight budget. Maybe your child gets sick and needs a trip to the doctor and some medicine. Perhaps a family member is involved in an accident and can't work for a few weeks. It could be that your car breaks down and you need it to get back and forth to work because you live too far out in the country for public transit.

These are the situations going on in more homes across the country every single day. It's simple to believe that the people suffering like this are just lazy, or not trying, or are spending frivolously. No one wants to think that these things can occur through no fault of the individual.

Why not?

Because that means *these things could also happen to them, too.*

Every time I write about crushing poverty, someone adds in the comments section a smug declaration about how people need to get an education, hang on to a job, buy cheaper food . . . there's a litany of condescending advice. If you're in the situation I'm describing, I know it's hard, but you have to let the criticism roll off of you.

PRIORITIZE YOUR PAYMENTS

The advice I have may not be popular, but let's talk about prioritizing your payments when you can't pay your bills. I am not promoting irresponsibility here. It's just math. When you have less money coming in than you have obligated to go out, you will not be able to pay all of your bills. It's that simple.

This list of priorities assumes that you have some money coming in, but not enough to meet your obligations. When things improve, you can try to catch up, but for now, you simply have to choose survival.

I suggest the following order of payments.

1. Pay for Shelter First

Your number one priority is keeping a roof over your head. That roof may not be the roof of the house you are in now, though, if your circumstances have changed and you can no longer afford it. If you can still manage to pay your rent/mortgage, do so in order to keep your family housed. If you rent, and your rent is a reasonable price, make this the first payment you make from your limited funds. You really, truly don't want to be homeless, and moving is expensive. Try your best to stay put.

If you own, consider your property taxes and insurance as part of your mortgage, because if you stop paying any of these, your home will be foreclosed on. If you can't pay your mortgage, property taxes, and insurance, you have a while before the home gets foreclosed on and you are forced to move out. If this is the case, it's *absolutely essential* that you put aside money for the place where you'll move should you have to leave your home. You're going to need first, last, and deposits in many cases, particularly since your credit isn't going to be stellar due to your financial situation. When you are in this situation, it can be difficult to force yourself to save money when so many things are being left unpaid, but if you ever hope to bail yourself out of this situation, you absolutely have to do this.

The laws vary from state to state,[5] but basically, this is the timeline:

---

5   http://www.nolo.com/legal-encyclopedia/free-books/foreclosure-book /chapter11-1.html.

- When you make the decision to let your house go back to the lender, you will have a month or two before they send you a notice of default.
- From that point, you usually have three months before the foreclosure proceedings begin. During those three months, you should be saving the money you would normally be putting toward your mortgage.
- At some point, you'll get a notice to vacate the premises.
- When this happens, you have two options. You can choose to move to a different home, or you can file for bankruptcy, if you feel your situation is such that there is absolutely no way out.
- If you file for bankruptcy, the home can't be resold by the lender for three more months, giving you more time to put aside money for your move.

Should we all pay the bills that we have promised to pay? Of course, we should. Our word is very important. Remember, though, that the information here is for people who are in a position in which they *do not have the money to pay*.

So, the bottom line is this: either pay your housing costs or put aside money for future housing as your first expenditure.

2. Buy Food

You have to eat, and so do your children. If you don't eat, you'll get sick, and then your situation will be even more dire.

- Stick to simple, wholesome basics and cook from scratch. Beans and rice have fed many a family.
- Tap into your inner Southerner and make inexpensive, filling meals like biscuits and gravy.
- Make soup to stretch just a few ingredients to feed a family.
- Save *all* of your leftovers, even the ones on people's plates. Add them to a container in the freezer and make a soup from that at the end of the week.

- Clean up after the potluck at church. Sometimes you can take home the leftovers.
- Don't skip meals to stretch your food further. You need your health and your strength to overcome this situation.
- Go to the library and check out a book on local edibles. Go foraging in the park or in nearby wooded areas.
- See if your grocery store sells out-of-date produce for use for animals. There's often a fair bit you can salvage and add to soups or casseroles. (This is the only way we were able to have vegetables and meat during one particularly painful stretch when my oldest daughter was young.)

In a worst-case scenario, food banks are an option as well.

3. Pay for Essential Utilities

You should be cutting your utility usage to the bare minimum and using every trick in the book to keep your bills as low as possible. If your utilities get shut off, it's going to be difficult to cook from scratch and you won't be able to keep leftovers from spoiling. You need the water running from your taps to drink, cook with, and clean. Depending on the climate and the season, heat may be vital as well.

If you can't pay the entire bill, call the utility companies and try to make payment arrangements. If your utilities are shut off, then you will have a hefty reconnection fee on top of the bill, which will be due in full.

Another point to remember is that our culture believes it's absolutely necessary that all homes be plugged in to the utility system. If you have a work-around, like wood heat and hand pumped well water, and decide that your utilities are not essential, you need to be prepared to face those whose opinions differ. Some cities have condemned homes which are not connected to the grid,[6] and if you have

---

6 http://www.thedailysheeple.com/florida-court-rules-off-grid-living -illegal_062015.

children who are of school age, sometimes a "concerned" teacher or neighbor has been known to report your situation to the child welfare authorities.[7]

4. Pay for Car/Work Necessities

What must you have in order to keep working? For me, it's the Internet, since I work online. All of my clients contact me via email and the work I do requires that I be able to send it to them and research things online. I live in the country, so driving to the library on a daily basis would cost more than my monthly Internet fees.

For another person, this necessity might be the cost of public transit or keeping their vehicle on the road so that they can get to work. Choose the least expensive options to keep yourself working but maintain your job-related necessities.

5. Pay for Anything Else

After you've paid all of the above, if you have money left over, now is the time to pay your other expenses. These expenses include debt that you've incurred or contracts you are involved in (like cell phone plans, etc.). Choose very carefully how you dole out any remaining money.

- Keep one phone going, with the lowest possible payment. This is necessary for work, for your children or their school to contact you in the event of an emergency, and as a contact point for your financial situation. Compare the cost of a cell phone, landline, or VOIP phone. Every family member does not require a phone, you just need one. (I actually did go for a couple of years with no phone at all, but I'm uniquely antisocial and had email by which I could be reached.)

---

7   http://www.thedailysheeple.com/police-seize-10-children-from-off-grid
    -homeschool-family_052015.

- If it's at all possible, try to use the snowball method discussed previously to pay off your debts and bail yourself out of your situation. Being without debt will allow you to live a much freer life in the future.
- If paying off debt is not possible, try to make the minimum payments.
- If the minimum payments are not possible, you may have to default, at least temporarily, on debts.
- Buy some pantry staples. If you can add some extra rice or cans of tomatoes to the pantry, it will help see you through this tight situation.
- Be relentless in deciding what will be paid and what will not. This is not the time for arguments like, "But it's our only form of entertainment" or "We deserve this one luxury." Cut all non-essentials until things improve.
- Focus on the most frugal options possible.

Things will get better And, if you are in a situation in which you can't pay your bills, I'm sorry.

I'm sorry about . . .

- The embarrassment you feel when you can't afford to meet someone for coffee.
- The sick feeling of seeing the bills pile up on the counter and not being able to do anything about it.
- The knot in your stomach every time the phone rings and it's a 1–800 number that you *know* is a bill collector.
- The stress of knowing you can't remain in your home.
- The fear that someone will say you aren't taking care of your kids and they'll be taken away.
- The humiliation when people don't understand and think it's all your fault.
- The hopelessness of watching the bank account empty out the day your pay goes in, and still having a dozen things unpaid.

- The overwhelming discouragement of having fees assessed on top of debts you already can't pay.
- The anxiety over what tomorrow will bring.

It *will* get better. You'll find a way to make it work. You just have to survive while you make it happen. Maybe you will pool your resources with another family, or get a raise, or find a cheaper place. But *you will find a way*.

Life may not be exactly as it was before, but it will be good again.

HOW TO EAT FROM THE PANTRY WHEN THERE'S NO MONEY FOR GROCERIES

When people hear the question, "How long could you survive on the food you have on hand?" they tend to think of the math. "I have 472 servings of grain divided by 4 people and . . ."

Stop.

You need to think in terms of meals. Those who think in individual components like this are the ones who will end up near the end of the pantry stretch eating canned peaches, stale saltines, and pureed pumpkin for dinner. Not the most enticing combo, right?

One really great way to stock up and have familiar food on hand is to think about seven meals that your family enjoys. Then, purchase for your pantry the ingredients for four of each of those meals. Here are a few quick tips.

- Look for non-perishable options, like freeze-dried mushrooms and bell peppers for your spaghetti sauce.
- Repackage meat carefully for your freezer in meal-sized servings.
- Learn how to make baked goods from scratch and stock up on the ingredients you need for them.
- Keep fruit and veggies on hand in frozen, dehydrated, and canned form.

- Have some quick meals on hand so that you don't end up breaking the budget on takeout food on a super busy day. (I pressure-can entire meals for this very reason.)
- Use emergency food to extend a small number of leftovers to feed the whole family.

PANTRY-FRIENDLY ADAPTATIONS

Lots of folks say things like "I only buy fresh XXX at the store, everything else came from the pantry." That's awesome, truly, but if you were in a situation in which you couldn't buy fresh XXX, you probably wouldn't want to go without it, right? Here are some things to stockpile so that you can make adaptations to fresh XXX.

- **Milk:** Powdered milk
- **Bread:** Stock up on the ingredients to make it yourself. Store-bought bread is usually loaded with additives so learning to bake your own is a worthy skill regardless of whether you intend to survive from your pantry.
- **Fresh fruit:** Frozen fruit is pretty yummy. In fact, my (slightly odd) kids enjoy gnawing on it right out of the freezer. You can also use it in smoothies, thaw and top yogurt or pancakes with it, or bake with it. We are huge applesauce fans, so I can a few dozen jars of this each fall. I also can peach and pear slices in honey for a sweet treat and loads of homemade jam which can be used in a multitude of ways that do not include toast.
- **Salad:** If you have a sunny windowsill you can grow salad greens all year long to sate your craving for fresh greens. There are lots of delicious microgreen kits on the market, and even some kits that are soil-free. Other alternatives are home-canned coleslaw or lightly cooked veggie salads made from freezer vegetables.
- **Vegetables:** You really don't have to have fresh asparagus in February, contrary to what the grocery stores portray. While I do can some vegetables, canned veggies are *not* my

favorite. I prefer fresh cooked al dente. The closest I can get to that with my food storage is frozen veggies, lightly steamed. I also keep dehydrated and freeze-dried veggies on hand for cooking with: mushrooms, bell peppers, onions, etc. If you have a root cellar, lots of good veggies can be stored there.

SAMPLE MENUS FROM OUR FOOD STORAGE PANTRY

Here are some of the meals I've created from my pantry and freezer.

Breakfasts

- We have an unlimited supply of eggs with ten hens laying enthusiastically, so most breakfasts center around them. Even if you don't have fresh eggs, you can purchase them fairly inexpensively as a staple of your diet.
- Omelets with leftover veggies from the night before and a bit of cheese sauce to make our cheese go further
- Eggs with sausage or bacon (we recently bought half a hog, so we have plenty of that)
- Homemade pancakes topped with fruit syrup made from home-canned jam
- Homemade granola or granola cookies
- Eggs and roasted veggies (One of our weird favorite breakfasts)
- Oatmeal topped with warmed jam
- Homemade bread (or cornbread) and jam
- Smoothies

Lunches

In our house, lunch is often leftovers from the night before. I usually try to cook enough for this very purpose. We do have some other standbys, though.

- Homemade chicken strips from the freezer with oven fries
- Beef patty with oven-baked carrot "fries"

- Roasted veggies topped with parmesan cheese
- Soup (all kinds: chicken, beef and vegetable, creamy cauliflower)
- Refried beans and rice topped with home-canned salsa
- Top a pizza crust or tortillas with home-canned pizza sauce, toppings that are leftovers, and cheese from the freezer
- Yogurt topped with fruit from the freezer and homemade granola

Dinners

The Crock-Pot gets a whole lot of use in my house. I love the fact that the meal is almost completely hands off while I'm busy doing other things. Of course, not all our recipes are Crock-Pot ones! Here are some of the dinners we have had over the past couple of weeks.

- Roast beef and vegetables (Crock-Pot)
- Carnitas (pork roast slow cooked with green tomato salsa, lime juice, and cilantro)
- Spaghetti and meatballs
- Pasta primavera with veggies from the freezer
- Stir fry from the freezer
- Pork chops and roasted vegetables sprinkled with parmesan
- Beef BBQ (Crock-Pot) and home-canned sweet and sour coleslaw
- Rice pilaf and brown rice cooked, then stir-fried with a small amount of leftover meat and egg to make a tasty bowl of fried rice
- Roasted chicken and vegetables
- Baked beans with gluten free mac and cheese
- Beef and vegetable stew
- Homemade chili (Crock-Pot)
- Split pea soup made with home-canned ham broth
- Potato soup (it's a family favorite and super thrifty!)
- And of course, no list of frugal meals would be complete without breakfast for dinner.

Chapter 12

HOW TO SURVIVE AN ECONOMIC CRISIS

Greece. Zimbabwe, Argentina, and Venezuela specifically come to mind when people think of countries who have seen hyperinflation and total economic collapse. And if you've payed attention to those grim situations, you know it isn't impossible that such a fate could befall your own country one day.

This chapter discusses how to survive situations like a stock market crash, a nationwide economic collapse, and hyperinflation and scarcity.

WHAT TO DO IN THE EVENT OF A STOCK MARKET CRASH

Has anyone noticed how the stock market has been extremely volatile? And how nearly everyone is soothed when industry specialists scramble to prop up our failing economy? It's not only happening in America; all over the globe, markets have been up and down more than usual. The last time the system showed this much volatility, the crash of 2008 occurred.

When markets slowly freefall and no one in the media is talking about it, that means it's time to sit up, pay attention, and be prepared to take immediate action.

TAKE THESE IMMEDIATE STEPS IF THE MARKET CONTINUES TO FALL

When things become extremely volatile, it's time to watch the market. Carefully. Like it's your job. If it continues to fall, we could all be in big trouble. It doesn't matter if you are invested in the market or not, we'll *all* be affected by a crash.

If the market continues to plummet, it's time to take action immediately. None of these steps will have long-term consequences if things level out, but they could make your life a whole lot easier if things get worse.

Here's what you need to do *immediately* in the event of a stock market crash.

- **Take your money out of the bank ASAP.** If you still keep your money in the bank, go there and remove as much as you can while leaving in enough to pay your bills. Although it wasn't a market collapse in Greece recently, the banks did close and limit ATM withdrawals. People went for quite some time without being able to access their money but were able to have a sense of normalcy by transferring money online to pay bills or using their debit cards to make purchases. **Get your cash out.** You don't want to be at the mercy of the banks.

- **Stock up on supplies.** Make sure you are prepped. If you're behind on your preparedness efforts and need to do this quickly, you can order buckets of emergency food just to have some on hand. (Hit the grocery store or wholesale club and stock up there, too, on your way home.)

- **Load up on fuel.** Fill up your gas tank and fill your extra cans also. Quite often, fuel prices skyrocket in the wake of a market crash.

- **Be prepared for the potential of civil unrest.** If the banks put a limit on withdrawals, (or close like they did in Greece) you can look for some panic to occur. If the stores dramatically increase prices or close, then more people will panic. Be armed and be prepared to stay safely at home. See the chapter on How to Survive Civil Unrest (pg. 83) for more information.

- **Be prepared for the possibility of being unable to pay your bills.** If things really go downhill, the middle class and those who are the working poor will be the most strongly affected, as they have been in Greece[1] during that country's financial crisis.

It may not happen, but you should always be ready for our next Great Depression. Be prepared to take action. This may just be a warning bell, but we all know that it's only a matter of time until we're all out of warnings.

VENEZUELA: A CAUTIONARY TALE

First, let's quickly look at the history of the collapse of Venezuela that has taken place over a period of years to know what we might expect.

- In 2013, many began to suspect that the outlook for Venezuela was grim when prepping became illegal. The Attorney General of Venezuela, Luisa Ortega Díaz,[2] called on prosecutors to target people who were "hoarding" basic staples with serious sanctions.
- Shortly thereafter, grocery stores instituted a fingerprint registry[3] to purchase food and supplies. Families had to register and were allotted a certain amount of supplies to prevent "hoarding."
- Then, in early 2015, it became even more apparent that the country was falling when long lines for basic necessities such as laundry soap, diapers, and food became the norm rather

1   https://www.theorganicprepper.com/how-austerity-will-increase-poverty-in-greece.
2   https://www.theorganicprepper.com/could-prepping-become-illegal-here-too-venezuelan-govt-to-detain-hoarders.
3   https://www.theorganicprepper.com/venezuela-enforces-fingerprint-registry-to-buy-groceries-what-to-do-before-rationing-starts-in-america.

than the exception.[4] Thousands of people were standing in line for five to six hours in the hopes that they would be able to purchase a few much-needed items.

- Shortly after the story broke to the rest of the world, the propaganda machine shifted into high gear. As the government began to ration electricity[5] in May 2015, it was announced that this was not due to economic reasons at all, but instead was a measure of their great concern for the environment.

- By July 2015, the situation continued to devolve, and farmers in Venezuela were forced[6] to hand over their crops from the summer. The government assumed control of essential goods like food and began putting retail outlets out of business. Then, once they had control of the sales outlets, they began forcing farmers and food manufacturers to sell anywhere from 30 to 100 percent of their products to the state at the price the state opted to pay, as opposed to stores and supermarkets.

- But that wasn't enough to keep the population fed. (Isn't it astonishing how much less motivated people are to produce food and supplies when they are no longer allowed to benefit from their hard work?) In January 2016, the government told citizens that they would need to produce their own food.[7] The Ministry of Urban Farming was created to oversee this. While self-reliance sounds great, it isn't so great in Venezuela. Just so the urban farmers didn't get *too* self-reliant, a registry

---

4   https://www.theorganicprepper.com/this-is-what-a-real-life -economic-collapse-looks-like.

5   https://www.theorganicprepper.com/case-study-in-collapse-propaganda -venezuela-is-now-rationing-electricity/.

6   https://www.theorganicprepper.com/government-of-venezuela-forces -farmers-to-hand-over-food.

7   http://latino.foxnews.com/latino/money/2016/01/21/venezuelas-response -to-food-shortages-grow-your-own-food-at-home/.

of the crops and livestock were to be required. (And obviously, they've already proven that they have no issue forcing farmers to hand over what they've produced.)

- The price of food soared as hyperinflation struck the country. A scant amount of groceries cost two weeks' salary for many Venezuelans.

But all of the socialist measures and forced food production weren't enough to keep the people of Venezuela fed. The Venezuelan government could no longer cover up the country's woes with propaganda. In February of 2017, the announcement of a "nutritional emergency" made it official. Venezuela was out of food, and the starvation of Venezuelans soon followed.[8] By 2018, the collapse was in full effect and Venezuelans were migrating out of the country in a mass exodus to escape the starvation, crime, and social decay.

HERE'S A CRASH COURSE ON HYPERINFLATION

Hyperinflation is when prices increase to ridiculous amounts very quickly, and it usually happens when a country's currency becomes worthless due to economic collapse or deficit spending, after the government prints more money that is backed by nothing. Hyperinflation nearly ruined Zimbabwe after the government unrestrainedly printed money to fight a war. It reached a staggering 2.2 million percent increase. The most famous case of hyperinflation occurred in the Weimar Republic of Germany in 1922–1923. In this case, hyperinflation reached 1,000,000,000,000 to 1. By 2017 in Venezuela, the price of food had reached astronomical proportions. The cost of a dozen eggs was equivalent to $45 USD in the store and $150 USD from the black market. Dry milk reached $75 to $100 USD per pound, and corn flour reached nearly $10 USD

---

8   https://www.theorganicprepper.com/venezuela-is-out-of-food-heres
-what-an-economic-collapse-really-looks-like/.

per pound.[9] Let me repeat one key point: Hyperinflation occurs due to economic collapse and when the government prints too much worthless money. Sound familiar?

How would financial collapse affect you?

Maybe you aren't an investor. Maybe you don't have real estate. Maybe you're absolutely certain, without a shadow of a doubt, that your job is secure. Perhaps you have money in the bank.

The trouble is, the money you are working overtime to make, the security you feel that you have by saving it . . . it's imaginary. It works for now, in our current system, but it's backed by nothing but debt and, in a crisis, will be worthless. Joshua Krause of *The Daily Sheeple* wrote[10] about the dollar:

> *But what is it* [money] *really worth?*
>
> *Nothing. It's worthless, and that's the godawful truth. I'm not exaggerating to make a point either. It's not just overrated, overinflated and backed by nothing but confidence. It is quite literally worthless. Less than worthless in fact! Our fractional reserve banking system spews out "money" that is nothing of the kind.*
>
> *This thing that we spend our whole lives desperately trying to accumulate; that builds our roads, feeds our bellies, pays our mortgages and fuels our dreams. This glorified token that puts our kids through school so that they may spend their whole lives trying to accumulate it as well, is not really money. It's debt! And it's not even your debt. It's somebody else's liability.*

Not only is your money worthless, here are a few more ways the current economic trends may still affect you.

---

9   https://www.theorganicprepper.com/what-food-costs-in-venezuela
    -eggs-150-a-dozen-dry-milk-100-a-pound/.

10   http://www.thedailysheeple.com/the-terrible-truth-about-the-money-in
    -your-pocket_122014#sthash.lryHJsoV.dpuf.

- **Prices will go up.** We've seen an almost unprecedented increase in the price of food over the past few years, even as the quality of the food available plummets. This is due to massive droughts, early freezes, and basic cost-of-living increases. Even if it doesn't reach hyperinflation levels, when you couple this with lower income, you have a problem.
- **Unemployment will ripple through the country.** Those without jobs now will be joined by others as businesses close and jobs are delegated to computers.
- **Rents will increase.** If you don't own your home, prepare to pay higher rent as landlords try to cover their losses of income in other sectors. Foreclosures will be on the rise, which means there will also be fewer homes available.

The bottom line is, income will remain the same, decrease, or even disappear entirely for many people. Meanwhile, the price of practically everything will go up. Expect to pay more for things like keeping your utilities on, feeding and clothing your family, and keeping a roof over your heads.

Aside from that, those dollars you are carefully saving? They are only providing you with the illusion of security. While right now we definitely need an emergency fund for those sudden catastrophes that pop up, you also need to focus on tangible items for a long-term, regional crisis.

How about another refresher on recent history? Remember the economic collapse in Greece? People were digging through garbage to find food. Suicides were rampant as people discovered that they literally could not afford to stay alive. Desperate parents gave up their children to orphanages, just in the hopes that their kids might be able to survive. This isn't something that happened in the distant past. This occurred in a beautiful, apparently thriving European country starting back in 2008.

If you ever prepped for anything that "might" happen, please understand that this current rate of spiral can only end one way: a financial collapse. There is a much greater statistical likelihood of your family suffering from the effects of this than being subject to a nuclear disaster, an EMP strike, or a devastating natural disaster. I'm not saying that these other things won't happen, but the odds are much greater that you will be affected by the economy.

You *must* prep before it happens.

PAY ATTENTION TO VENEZUELA

The best way to make your supply list is to figure out what the citizens of Venezuela ran out of first. Below, you can find a list of the things they ran out of first, along with suggestions for stocking up or educating yourself.

Even if we never have a problem in the United States, you can rest assured that none of these supplies are crazy things you'll never use. Most are the most basic of necessities and you'll find it's very convenient to be able to "shop in your pantry" whenever you need something. Learning to be more self-reliant is a great way to save money, live simpler, and often be healthier than those who depend on the store to meet all their needs.

Food

Supplies mentioned in articles that people have stolen and waited all day in line for are dry milk, bread, chicken, rice, cornmeal, beans, and flour.

Here's a list of food and related supplies you should stock up on.

- **Long-term emergency food buckets:** They're packed in square containers for easy stacking at the back of your closet, and each container is a month of food for one person. You can build up quite a stockpile this way that doesn't take up a lot of space. It's packaged to last for up to thirty years, so you can get it and forget it.
- **Build a pantry:** Purchase things on sale to build your first line of defense against food instability. (Always check the

expiration dates.) The pantry you build today can help you weather difficult times in the future. Stock up on shelf-stable versions of the things you generally consume in your family. You want to create at least a couple of months' supplies where you can supplement what you get at the store, with what you have in your kitchen cupboards. Be sure to focus on pantry staples so that you can combine ingredients for delicious, scratch meals.

- **Milk:** One of the first things people run out of is milk. If your family regularly drinks milk, or if you add it to your coffee, the lack of it is something that will be immediately evident and make them feel deprived in an already unsettling situation. You can freeze milk when it's on sale, and you should also stock up on shelf-stable dry milk. That's the best way to have it on hand for the long haul.

Hygiene Items

It's important to be able to remain clean if you want to stay healthy. Following are some of the supplies that have been in shortage in Venezuela for months now.

- Soap
- Laundry detergent
- Toilet paper
- Diapers
- Feminine hygiene supplies

For some of these items, you can learn to make them yourself. For others, you can make or purchase reusable versions.

Medicine and Medical Care

The real nitty gritty of the situation in Venezuela is that a hospital visit is just as likely to kill you as make you better now, due to terrible sanitation and a lack of supplies. They're out of antibiotics, cancer medicine, and equipment. They can't do dialysis or other life-saving treatments. They have no running water, so they're doing operations on a table still covered with blood from the last patient. The rolling blackouts mean that every single day, babies and other patients dependent on respirators are dying. Doctors are making lists of supplies for the families of patients to go out and attempt to procure from the black market.

It is essential that you keep some supplies on hand, and that you begin learning all you can about survival and herbal medicine.

- Stock up on over-the-counter medications for pain relief, allergies, colds, diarrhea, and inflammation.
- Some people purchase veterinary antibiotics and medications.
- Create a kit of wound treatment supplies to help prevent infection.
- I'm a huge fan of Vetricyn. We spray it on human wounds as well as animal ones.
- Take every class you can on first aid, paramedic skills, and herbalism.
- Create a reference library so that you can figure out how to deal with medical issues if help is not available.

In a long-term situation, it is very clear that stockpiling will not be enough. No matter how many cans of green beans you have stored away, one day they will run out. We have become so dependent on the "buy it as you need it" lifestyle that despite our food storage, there are still gaps that must be filled. And the only way to fill these gaps is through that which is a step beyond prepping . . . self-sufficiency.

SELF SUFFICIENCY

Self-sufficiency is defined as the ability to provide for oneself without the help of others. No amount of stockpiling gives you true self sufficiency. It is a combination of skills, supplies, attitudes, and habits that mean the difference between a person with a great pantry and a true survivor.

Self-sufficiency is for . . .

- The day the grocery stores close their doors or become so expensive that people cannot afford to shop.
- The day that the banks go on an indefinite holiday, after draining depositor savings accounts and pension funds.
- The day that electricity and heat on demand become so expensive that only the wealthy can afford them.
- The day that medical care no longer exists for the average person.
- The day that a natural disaster or false flag locks down the country and completely, irrevocably changes our way of life.

Self-sufficiency, unlike prepping, doesn't cost a lot of money, it's about planning and acquiring basic skills and tools. It is about putting your plan into practice before you have no other option but to do so. What would you do if you could never go to a store again? If you could never have utilities provided by a supplier again? What if you were truly on your own, forever? For some situations, prepping just isn't enough. If you don't have plans for the following, you cannot consider yourself to be truly prepared.

Water
Clean drinking water is one of the most important requirements for survival. Now is the time to figure out how you will get water if your stored water runs out. Some ideas might be:

- Rain barrels (which are beginning to be illegal in some states)
- Less obvious water collection containers like pools and ponds (don't forget the roof if you live in an apartment building)
- Water purification methods

- Nearby lakes, rivers, and streams
- Wells (including non-electric pumps)

Food Production

Many people believe that they will just be able to stick some seeds in the ground and feed their families year-round. It isn't that easy. You can only learn the foibles of your bit of ground through trial and error. It takes a lot more veggies than most people think to feed a family for a year. Anything from a blight to bad weather to a horde of hungry bunnies can wipe out all your hard work and leave you without a bite to store away. Look into some of these methods:

- Gardening in your backyard or on a balcony
- Aquaponics or hydroponics systems
- Raising chickens and other micro-livestock
- Sprouting
- Hunting and foraging (a nice supplement to your diet but a risky plan for long term survival when everyone else has the same idea)
- Full-scale farming
- Rooftop gardening
- Greenhouses and cold-frames

Make sure to stock up on gardening supplies and tools. Once everyone wants them, the price will skyrocket. Stock up now on seeds, tools, compost bins, soil amendments, and soil testing kits.

And if you live in an apartment, *learn to garden in an apartment.*

I frequently suggest that people take more steps toward self-reliance and there are always folks who say, "That's fine for you, you live in the country. I can't grow food in an apartment." Well, you should probably figure out how to grow food in an apartment, because in Venezuela, President Maduro's suggestion that people grow food didn't have the caveats of "if it's convenient and you live in the country."

I understand that you can't raise all your food in a tiny apartment with a postage stamp balcony, but you can raise some things. Lettuce for salads, sprouts that can be used in numerous ways, or if you're really industrious, you could try aquaponics and/or rabbits. Everything you manage to produce can help supplement the meager rations you may be forced to live on.

Food Preservation

Not all of us are lucky enough to live in a place where we can grow food outdoors all year long. For the rest of us, food preservation is a lifeline in the winter. Only a few basic supplies and tools are needed. Just like food production, it's important to practice food preservation and work out the kinks now, while you still have moderately affordable groceries as a backup. This also allows you to rely on healthy, non-GMO foods instead of the inexpensive, highly processed garbage at the stores.

Learn the following skills:

- Canning
- Freezing
- Dehydrating/drying
- Pickling
- Fermentation
- Salting and curing
- Root cellaring

Reduce Dependence on Utilities

During a long-term collapse, utilities can be rationed or cut out entirely. This affects everyday life, in that food can't be kept in freezers, you'll likely wind up dealing with hot humid weather without air conditioning, cold weather without central heating, and nights without electric lighting.

Whether you live in the country or in a high-rise apartment, you need to take steps to reduce your dependency on electricity at the flip of a switch, water from the tap, heat from the thermostat, and cooking at the turn of a dial. As the divide between the rich and the poor widens, there could one day be a choice between food and electricity.

Your priorities are:

- Water
- Sanitation
- Heat
- Electrical power
- Lights
- Refrigeration or other method of safe food storage
- Cooking methods

Every situation is unique so start now to amass the necessary tools to meet your needs should the lights go out on a long-term basis.

Personal Defense

When people become more desperate, they become more willing to do things they'd never have considered in better times. Not only do you need to know how to protect your family and property, you need to make it less attractive to those who are doing without.

- Make your property less accessible by fencing it
- Install heavy doors in reinforced frames
- Install sturdy brackets to hold a bar in place on either side of the doors
- Grow thorny inhospitable plants under windows and on fences
- Place alarms on windows and doors
- Install security cameras (even if they are fake and just have a blinking light)
- Keep a low profile, if no one else has lights or power, cover your windows thoroughly so that they cannot see that you have them

- Don't be ostentatious, keep your property looking similar to everyone else's in your neighborhood
- Keep all windows and doors securely locked
- Consider the potential necessity of standing watch in shifts if the situation has thoroughly devolved

I'm not suggesting that you stop prepping. Your stockpile is vital insurance that can help to cushion you when things go downhill, but along with your food storage and your rocket stoves and your medical supplies, begin creating a self-sufficient lifestyle that will carry you far beyond what mere prepping ever could.

Appendix 1
PANIC PREPPING BASICS

The following section is a reference for prepping basics. I referred to these basics throughout the book and they give more detailed information on the specific topics. If you're brand-spanking new to prepping and a disaster is drawing near, you're going to want to get ready in a hurry. This section is for you! This may not cover *all* of your bases, but it will get you through at least a short-term disaster. Nearly all of these supplies will be easily available at your local discount or hardware store. A better option, of course, would be to pick up these items ahead of time and have an emergency kit sitting there ready when a storm is bearing down. But we can work on that.

Other appendices will have more details for when you have more time to get serious about things. For now, let's get to it!

WATER SUPPLY

Many events over the past years have taught us that a water emergency can happen to anyone. If your area suffers from tainted tap water, you'll want to have a backup supply on hand to keep your family (including pets) hydrated. This does not mean buying a case of twenty-four water bottles.

The thriftiest quick option is to purchase those one-gallon water jugs that are about $1 at the store. Get a supply that will last for two weeks, one per day, per family member. That will cost approximately $14 per family member. However, if you wait too long, the water will be gone. You can also bottle and store your tap water, but if you're not really into the whole idea of prepping, you may not want to put forth the effort to do this. You can also buy and fill five-gallon water jugs at the store, but be aware that your electric water dispenser may not work if the power is out, particularly if it is bottom-fed.

HEAT

This is essential in colder climates. Lack of heat can cause people to make bad choices—sometimes deadly ones—by using methods that can cause a build-up of carbon monoxide.

If you're lucky, you may have a wood burning fireplace or wood stove. If you have that, simply make sure you have enough wood to burn for a while. You may also have a natural gas fireplace. Most of the time, these will work when the power goes out, although they won't have a blower and will only thoroughly heat one room.

An excellent secondary heater is the Mr. Buddy propane heater. You can attach this to a barbecue propane tank. This heater is rated for indoor use (in most states). Have the correct attachments and keep at least two tanks of propane on hand to see you through an emergency.

Be prepared to close off one room where there is a heat source. You can use curtains or quilts in doorways for this, or if the room has doors, stuff towels under them to keep the heat from escaping.

Always have a battery-operated carbon monoxide detector. Your life could quite literally depend on it.

SANITATION SUPPLIES

Good hygiene is even more important during a disaster. Food and water borne illnesses can be deadly.

- Paper towels
- Bleach wipes
- Baby wipes
- Hand sanitizer
- Supplies to make a kitty litter toilet for humans (See instructions in Appendix 6 on page 185)

- Bleach
- Disposable rags for cleaning up
- Heavy duty trash bags

LIGHTS

When the lights go out, you'll want to have backup lighting. That scented candle in the middle of your coffee table isn't going to last for days and days.

- Buy tea lights. They are safe and inexpensive.
- Don't forget lighters and matches!
- Bring in your solar garden stakes at night for a cozy glow. You can often find these at the dollar store.
- Pick up some glow bracelets for the kiddos. This is a safe way to give them some light in their bedrooms.
- Be sure to have flashlights and extra batteries on hand.

A WAY TO COOK

Even if you have loads of food in your pantry, it won't help you much if you have no way to cook it. Here are a few options.

- If you have a gas stove, it will probably work during most power outages. A great way to test this is to simply throw the breaker and make certain it still comes on. Some stoves have an electric ignition and will not turn on without being manually lit.
- A backyard barbecue is another thing that most folks already have on hand that can pull double duty during an emergency. Mine also has a burner.
- An emergency stove that can be used indoors. Make sure it is rated for indoor use and don't forget to have plenty of extra fuel for it. (I use the Bobcat stove.)
- A Kelly Kettle is a popular rocket stove that can use any type of biomass to boil water quickly.

- A camp stove is another excellent option. Coleman is a trusted name, and these can be found in any store with a camping/outdoors department. Be sure that you have enough propane to last for three meals per day for a couple of weeks.

FOOD SUPPLY

Finally, you need a food supply, and it needs to be shelf-stable. During a longer power outage, the items in your refrigerator will spoil fairly quickly, and eating something that could make you sick is even less of a good idea during an emergency. There are numerous options.

- Buy some buckets. Buckets of food are generally considered a one-month supply for one person. The fastest, easiest way to build a food supply for emergencies is to pick up a bucket for each member of the family.
- Stock up on canned soups, stews, fruits, and vegetables. These will last a long time on a basement shelf and can be heated up very quickly to conserve your fuel.
- Get canned meat: tuna, salmon, chicken, and ham are all readily available. Don't forget to keep a couple of manual can openers on hand.
- Consider no-cook options. If you don't have a secondary cooking method, look to things like peanut butter and crackers, dried fruit, canned veggies, and tortillas.
- Protein powder is a good option to make a filling, tasty beverage (a lot of emergency food is fairly low on protein.)
- Keep dry milk on hand for coffee, cereal, and drinking.
- Skip the beans and rice if they aren't already prepared. Unless you are cooking them over the fire in your fireplace, you are going to use far too much fuel to prepare stuff like that from scratch. Focus on foods that can be reheated or prepared in less than twenty minutes.

The most important thing to remember here is not to rely on the things in your fridge and freezer during a lengthy power outage. You want to eat those things for the first day or so, working from fridge to freezer, but after that, you need to switch to shelf-stable mode. It's wise not to intermingle your emergency supplies with your other supplies. The particularly tasty things will get used up and you'll be left eating saltines and canned peaches. Not fun. Pick up one to two large plastic tubs and keep the majority of your supplies in them. Not your propane though, you will want to ensure that propane is stored correctly.[1]

DISPOSABLES

It may not be green, but the last thing you're going to want to deal with during a power outage in which you may not have hot water, is washing tons of dishes or laundry. Pick up some disposable items to have on hand for basic sanitation:

- Paper plates
- Paper cups
- Plastic flatware
- Napkins
- Paper towels
- Cleaning wipes

TOOLS AND SPECIAL SUPPLIES

This will vary depending on your disaster, but here are some basics.

- Plywood
- Screws
- Fully charged screwdriver and manual backups
- Duct tape

---

1   http://www.silive.com/homegarden/homeimprovement/index.ssf /2009/03/play_it_safe_learn_how_to_hand.html.

- Tarps
- Bug spray and insect repellant

SPECIAL NEEDS ITEMS

These items will vary from family to family, but this list should trigger some ideas. Think about the things your family members use and need on a frequent basis.

- Prescription medications (probably the most vital thing on the list)
- Over-the-counter medications
- Antihistamines
- Diapers and baby wipes
- Hair elastics (ask any woman with long hair how essential this is!)
- Lip balm
- Sunscreen
- Hand lotion

Keep it all together. I can't encourage you enough to buy these things ahead of time. When an emergency is pending, everyone else will be out there with the same idea. As for getting prepped at the last minute, hey, better late than never! Welcome to the prepped side!

Appendix 2

EMERGENCY FOOD BASICS

What should you eat during an emergency?

Well, there are as many answers to that question as there are people reading this. Every one of us will have different requirements. So, use the information in this section as a general guideline, but don't be afraid to veer from it if your circumstances require you to do so.

Here are some things to consider when deciding what emergency food will work best for your family:

- Do you have any food allergies or intolerances in the family? (A food reaction can make an already stressful situation far worse!)
- Do you have any special dietary needs in your family such as low sodium for someone with high blood pressure or low carb for someone with diabetes?
- Do you have a specific way of eating? Try to stick as closely to your normal diet as possible. An abrupt change can cause lethargy, digestive upset, and illness.
- Do you have a way to cook the food if the power goes out? (If not, consider focusing on foods that don't require cooking)
- Does your off-grid cooking method require fuel that may be limited, like a fuel canister? (Focus on foods that cook quickly and will use less fuel.)
- Or is it the same one you're using to heat your house, like a wood stove, in which the fuel would be used anyway? (You

can cook things that have long cooking times, like dried beans and rice.)

- Do you have an abundant water supply for rehydrated freeze-dried food? (If not, you should consider focusing on canned foods instead of freeze-dried foods.)
- Do you have any extremely picky family members? (It's easy to scoff and say they'll eat if they're hungry enough, but again, the situation is already stressful and there's no need to make it worse!)

The questions and answers above can provide some guidelines for your stockpile.

BASIC FOOD LIST

This food list is per person and focuses on things that require less cooking. It will see you through a couple of weeks without power, give or take a little.

- 1 pound dry milk (This will make 14 cups of milk)
- ½ pound coffee (This will make 36 cups for an adult—be sure you have a French press for making it)
- ½ pound sugar (for coffee, cereal, etc.)
- 2 pounds pasta (8 servings)
- 4 pouches pre-cooked rice (8 servings)
- 2 jars/cans marinara sauce (8 servings)
- 6 cans tuna
- 6 cans chicken breast
- 1 jar peanut butter
- 2 boxes saltine crackers
- 1 box graham crackers
- 1 box breakfast cereal
- 1 box instant oatmeal (already flavored and sweetened will make life easier during an emergency)
- 4 cans soup
- 8 cans fruit

- 12 cans vegetables
- 14 individual cups pudding and/or applesauce
- 14 flour tortillas (Don't go organic with this. You're looking for shelf-stable)
- 2 cans refried beans
- 1 jar salsa (This will be enough for the whole family—you don't need 1 apiece)
- 1 box granola bars
- 1 package cookies or other shelf-stable treats
- Shelf-stable parmesan cheese
- 2 bottles fruit juice
- Dried fruit

I also save condiments from times when we get takeout or grab a meal on the go for use during a power outage.

CREATIVE MEALS

Always use the things in your fridge first. If you have time on the first day, before things begin to spoil, use up the food in your fridge before you break into the emergency stash. Eat leftovers, combine things into new meals, and snack on cheese, fruit, and vegetables.

Then, mix and match the basic foods from the list above to make the following meals:

- Wraps or crackers with tuna or chicken
- Soup with crackers (stir in some rice or pasta to stretch it a bit further)
- Bean burritos
- Oatmeal with dried fruit
- Cereal with milk and dried fruit
- Pasta with marinara and parmesan
- Pasta with peanut sauce and veggies
- "Pizza" with a tortilla base, marinara sauce, and parmesan cheese

- Casserole with chicken, vegetables, and rice
- Peanut butter and crackers
- Peanut butter and graham crackers

To make life easier, keep the following disposable items on hand for use during an emergency.

- Paper plates
- Paper towels and napkins
- Plastic cutlery
- Baby wipes
- Disinfecting wipes
- Plastic cups

NO-COOK FOODS FOR POWER OUTAGES

If you don't have a secondary way to cook, many of the foods above will work without being heated up. Here are some of my family's favorite power outage no-cook meals. (Some are repeats of the menu above.)

1. Graham crackers with peanut butter
2. Protein shakes (I have a shaker cup with a whisk ball in it for this very purpose)
3. Saltines with peanut butter
4. Fresh fruit (apples, oranges, bananas)
5. Canned juice
6. Trail mix
7. Dry cereal
8. Cereal with rehydrated milk
9. Canned baked beans with ham or bacon
10. Pretzels
11. Nuts
12. Pudding cups
13. Canned fruit

14. Jerky
15. Pouches of pre-cooked and seasoned rice or quinoa
16. Cookies
17. Granola bars
18. Crackers
19. Dried fruits
20. Sandwiches: Peanut butter and jelly, tuna, leftovers from the fridge before they spoil

RECIPES . . . SORT OF

Following are some "recipes" for power outage food. Okay, "recipe" is a stretch, perhaps just some "tasty combinations."

- **No-Power Nachos**: Layer tortilla chips with canned cheese sauce, salsa, and canned jalapenos
- **S'mores:** Top graham crackers with chocolate-nut spread and marshmallow fluff
- **Wraps:** Soft tortillas filled with canned meat, a touch of mustard or mayo, and veggies from the fridge
- **No-Cook Tacos:** Hard tortillas with canned meat (we use our home canned chicken or taco meat for this), salsa, and canned cheese sauce
- **Main Dish Tuna Salad:** Combine a can of tuna, a can of white beans, chopped onion, chopped peppers, and chopped black olives (veggies are optional). Top with Italian dressing or mayo mixed with Dijon mustard to taste.
- **Pudding Cones:** Drain canned fruit of choice and stir it into vanilla pudding. Serve in ice cream cones for a kid-friendly treat. (We do this with yogurt also.)
- **Mexican Bean Salad:** Combine 1 can black beans, drained and rinsed, with 1 can corn, drained, and salsa to taste. For the dressing mix ½ jar salsa, ½ tsp each chili powder, onion powder, and garlic powder, and 3 tbsp lemon

juice. Toss well. Serve as a salad, in a soft tortilla, or mixed with a pouch of pre-cooked rice.

What if you have to go longer-term?

To take your food plan even further, consider ways that you can go long-term with food sustainability and cooking methods. Someday, if a disaster lasts long enough, your food supply will run out. It's a great idea to work on producing food self-reliantly well before you actually need it to survive.

A few suggestions are:

- Grow a garden and save your seeds
- Have a greenhouse or extend your growing season with cold frames and hoop houses
- Have a well-stocked pantry and a long-term food supply
- Have supplies for off-grid canning (jars, lids, outdoor burner)
- Learn ways to get by without refrigeration, like clay pot coolers, spring cooling,[1] and root cellaring
- Outdoor cooking methods such as charcoal barbecues, firepits, propane grills (and extra propane), and solar cookers
- Off-grid smokers can help you preserve meat
- Learn off-grid food drying techniques

---

1 https://www.brighthub.com/environment/green-living/articles/116158 .aspx.

Appendix 3
EMERGENCY WATER BASICS

Everyone knows that clean drinking water is something you can't live without. In the event of a disaster, the water may not run from the taps, and if it does, it might not be safe to drink, depending on the situation. If there is a boil order in place, remember that if the power is out, boiling your water may not be as easy as turning on your stove.

A water disaster can happen to anyone without warning.

- Maybe your car broke down in the desert and you have to wait or walk to find help.
- Maybe you didn't have the money to pay your water bill (or you just forgot to pay it) and it has been shut off for a few days.
- Maybe a nearby business has tainted municipal water in an industrial accident.
- Maybe the power went out and your home was on well water, thus halting your running water until the electricity can be restored.
- Maybe you were out hiking and got lost, then were forced to spend a few nights in the woods with only the supplies in your daypack.

Water preparedness should be one of your first priorities because water disasters are extremely common. You've probably heard the Prepper's Rule of 3:

- 3 minutes without air
- 3 days without water
- 3 weeks without food

While that isn't 100 percent accurate, if disaster strikes and you're still breathing (and not in imminent danger) you should immediately begin concentrating on a safe water supply.

Before the need for emergency water ever arises, you should create a four-level water preparedness plan.

1. Store
2. Acquire
3. Purify
4. Conserve

But first, you need to figure out how much water you really need. And it's probably a lot more than you think.

Just as no two families are the same, no two water plans are the same, either. Your plan will be dependent upon a wide array of variables.

- How many family members you have (or are expecting)
- Ages and health conditions of your group
- Where your home water comes from
- Available storage space
- Climate and weather conditions
- Natural resources on or near your property
- Financial situation

Standard prepper wisdom says that you need approximately one gallon per person per day, and that's a good starting point, but it isn't totally accurate. Things like hot weather, exertion, pregnancy, and illness can all increase the need for water. This also doesn't take into consideration the water you'll need for sanitation, pets, livestock, and gardens.

To get an accurate picture of how much water you need, you should try living without running water for a while. The best way to do this is to shut off the main to the house for a couple of days, grab a notebook, and find out how much water you *really* use.

Be sure to track:

- Drinking water
- Water you add to beverages (like brewed coffee or lemonade)
- Other beverages will count toward your hydration. If you drink a soda pop, count it toward your water usage.
- Water used for cleaning (washing dishes, wiping counters, etc.)
- Water used for personal hygiene (brushing teeth, washing hands, taking sponge baths, etc.)
- Water used for pets, gardens, and livestock
- Water used for cooking (pasta, rice, veggies, condensed soups, etc.)

You'll probably be surprised at how much you really use.

STORING WATER

While it is tempting to buy fresh, sealed bottles of water from the store, that can get pretty expensive. A good (and thrifty) way to start is by filling containers that you already have.

Good containers to use:

- 2-liter soda bottles
- Water bottles
- 5-gallon jugs
- PETE or PET plastic containers

Unsafe containers to use:

- Milk or juice jugs

- Containers that stored toxic items
- Containers that are not food-grade plastic

Here are FEMA's instructions[1] for safely storing water.

- Thoroughly clean the bottles with dishwashing soap and water, and rinse completely.
- For plastic soft drink bottles, sanitize by adding a solution of 1 teaspoon of non-scented liquid household chlorine bleach to a quart of water. Swish the sanitizing solution in the bottle so that it touches all surfaces.
- After sanitizing the bottle, thoroughly rinse out the sanitizing solution with clean water.
- Fill the bottle to the top with regular tap water. Note that if your water utility company treats your tap water with chlorine, you do not need to add anything else to the water to keep it clean. If the water you are using comes from a well or water source that is not treated with chlorine, add two drops of non-scented liquid household chlorine bleach to each gallon of water.
- Tightly close using the original cap. Don't contaminate the cap by touching the inside with your fingers.
- Write the date on the outside so that you know when you filled it. Store in a cool, dark place. Water that is properly stored will be safe for a year or longer.

While it's fine to carefully reuse containers for water storage, commercially bottled or canned water (sealed) is the best choice if you can afford it. It lasts indefinitely without the need for further purification.

ACQUIRING WATER

You've stored enough of the crystal-clear, life-sustaining liquid to keep your family hydrated and meet your household's needs for

---

1   https://www.fema.gov/txt/library/f&web.txt.

several weeks. But what if your supply runs dry? What if the unthinkable happens and you find you are down to the last few drops?

Well before the need arises, you need to know where to find water in your area. Some places you might find water for the long-term are:

- Creeks
- Rivers
- Lakes
- Ponds
- Natural springs
- Wells
- Rainwater collection

If you have a well or a spring for water, you'll be well off, but you need to remember a few important factors. Be sure that you have a way to get the water out of the well. Solar or manual pumps are your best options.

Also, keep in mind that any natural water source must be considered risky until proven otherwise. Pick up some testing kits to have on hand so that you can be certain that the water you're drinking is safe.

If you are getting your water from rivers, lakes, ponds, streams, and creeks, you must assume it is *not* safe to drink, as the possibilities for contaminants are virtually endless.

PURIFYING WATER

There are numerous ways to purify water. The method or methods you choose will depend on the water source, how much water you need to purify, and what kind of contaminants you may be dealing with.

Following, you'll find details on a few different methods of water purification, along with the pros and cons of each technique.

Boiling

Let water reach a full rolling boil for one full minute. If you're above 6,500 feet, add three minutes to your boiling time.

- Removes most pathogens, including protozoa, bacteria, and viruses
- Will not remove chemical contamination
- Will not remove pathogens from sewage
- If you boil too long, you will lose water to evaporation
- Not your best method if fuel is in short supply

Chemical Treatment

Chemical tablets and powders are all used differently, so follow instructions on the package.

- Water purification pills are a good portable option for your bug-out bag
- Water should be filtered first
- Works better on warm water
- Does not work on protozoa
- People with shellfish allergies may be allergic to iodine
- Iodine should not be used for more than 14 days to prevent toxicity
- Use only unscented chlorine bleach

Filtration Methods

Filtration methods strain out the solid impurities in the water.

- Activated carbon filters improve taste and odor and remove chemicals, gases, and some metals
- Activated carbon filters won't remove dissolved solids or most heavy metals
- If you don't replace the filter often enough, they can actually *add* bacteria to your water

- Other filtering elements are made of ceramic, glass fiber, hard-block carbon, or materials that resemble compressed surgical paper

Reverse Osmosis

Reverse osmosis (RO) forces water through a special membrane that allows water molecules through, but stops larger molecules like lead, chromium, and arsenic from getting past.

- RO removes total dissolved solids, asbestos, nitrates, radium, pesticides, chlorinated particles, copper, fluoride, and VOC (Volatile Organic Compounds)
- RO is also effective in eliminating bacteria, viruses, giardia lamblia, and cryptosporidium
- RO systems work slowly
- RO systems use about three times as much water as they treat, so they aren't ideal in situations when water availability is limited

Distillation

Distillers heat water to the boiling point and then collect the vapor as it condenses.

- Kills most disease-causing microbes and eliminates most chemical contaminants
- Contaminants that easily turn into gases (like gasoline and radon) may remain
- Natural minerals are also removed, which means you don't get their benefits
- It takes four to five hours to distill one gallon of water
- Distillation uses a great deal of both fuel and water

Ultraviolet Light

Ultraviolet (UV) light destroys disease-causing microorganisms by penetrating them and attacking their genetic core or DNA.

- UV purification does not use any chemicals or leave behind by-products
- One of the best ways to kill microbes
- UV units use very little energy and require little maintenance
- UV light does not eliminate contaminants like chlorine, heavy metals, and VOCs
- UV purification must be used in conjunction with another method

Gravity Filters

Some gravity filters contain elements that both purify and filter your water, making it completely ready to drink.

- Gravity filters do not require power to work
- Depending on the product, they can remove viruses, bacteria, and residual chlorine, and reduce heavy metals, VOCs, arsenic, and nitrites
- A high-quality gravity filter is an essential part of your water preparedness plan
- A portable gravity filter is an important addition to your EDC kit and bug-out bag

CONSERVING WATER

When water is in short supply or when you have to earn every drop by acquiring it and purifying it, you're going to want to treat it like the precious commodity that it is. Here are a few quick tips to use less water.

First, I'll refer back to the wisdom of my granny, who grew up having to manually pump the water for her family and carry it indoors. She never forgot those lessons, even decades after having running water in her home, and we can learn from her habits.

- Reuse cooking water
- Use a cup for shaving
- Use a pitcher and bowl for washing up
- Use a glass of potable water for toothbrushing
- Wash clothes in the leftover soapy water in the bathtub
- Wash produce in a basin
- Reuse gray water for flushing if you have a septic system
- If you have a garden, there are ways to conserve water there, too:
  - Harvest rainwater for the garden
  - Use an organic mulch to reduce the need for watering
  - Water early or late in the day
  - Landscape with local plants
  - Grow organic; chemical fertilizers increase the need for water

Get these supplies for a low-tech water plan.

A low-tech water plan might include some or all of the following:

- A manual pump for your well
- Buckets and wheelbarrows for hauling water from a nearby source
- Rain barrels for water harvesting
- A gravity-fed water filtration system
- A water dispenser for convenient access to filtered water (Be sure to get one with the bottle on top so that it can be operated without electricity, and not one that uses an electric pump to pull the water up from the bottom)
- Alternatively, you can get a hand pump for the top of the water bottle
- Storage units for water such as cisterns or tanks
- Portable water filters for safe water when you are away from home

WATER SAFETY

Did you know that the number one cause of death post-disaster is waterborne illnesses, like amoebic dysentery, shigellosis, hepatitis A, typhoid, cholera, and leptospirosis? That is because people get desperate when water is in short supply.

When you're thirsty—truly thirsty to the point that your body is beginning to suffer the effects of dehydration—you will drink whatever water is available, even when you know that it will likely make you ill. The need to quench your thirst and hydrate your body will override your brain's warnings that the water isn't safe. Don't let your family get that desperate. Create a water plan and understand the principles of safe water so that they never have to drink unsafe water to keep from dying from dehydration. Waterborne illness is truly miserable, in many cases causing severe vomiting and diarrhea. Common sense would suggest that you treat this with an anti-diarrheal like loperamide (Imodium) or diphenoxylate with atropine (Lomotil).

WATERBORNE ILLNESS

If someone becomes ill and you suspect they may be suffering from a waterborne illness, *do not* treat them with drugs to stop the diarrhea. They need to get the bacteria or virus out of their system and keeping it in their bodies can cause it to attack other organs.

Treat them for dehydration with plenty of filtered fluids and electrolytes and let the illness run its course otherwise.

Appendix 4

POWER OUTAGE SURVIVAL BASICS

To prepare for a month-long emergency, think about what you would need if the power went out and you couldn't leave your home for thirty days. Once you begin creating your plan, you may be surprised and discover that you already have most of what you need to batten down the hatches for a couple of weeks. It's just a matter of organizing so you can see what you need.

Use the following information to create your personal one-month preparedness plan. Modify the suggestions to adapt them to your particular home, family, and climate.

1. Begin by personalizing the suggestions to fit your family's needs and make a list of your requirements.
2. Next, do a quick inventory. As I mentioned above, you may be surprised to see that you already have quite a few of the recommended supplies.
3. Make a shopping list and acquire the rest of the items you need. If you can't afford everything right now, prioritize the most important things first.
4. Organize your supplies so that they are easily accessible when you need them.

You'll notice that I don't recommend lots of expensive gadgets that make prepping out of reach for ordinary families. Personally, I don't often invest in pricey generators or expensive equipment. Low-tech prepping is much more affordable and sustainable for those of us without extravagant budgets.

WATER

See Appendix 3 (pg. 157) for more information.

FOOD PREPARATION

There are two schools of thought regarding food during a power outage. One: you need a cooking method that does not require the grid to be functioning. Two: you can store food that doesn't require cooking. If you opt for a secondary cooking method, be sure that you have enough fuel for two weeks. See Appendix 2 (pg. 151) for more information.

HEAT

Homes these days aren't built to function without a connection to the power grid. If you aren't fortunate enough to live in an older home that was designed for off-grid living, look at some ways to take your home back a century or so. A secondary heating system is vital in most climates.

- An antique oil heater can use lots of different oils and is usually easy to install
- Have a wood stove installed
- Clean your chimney and get your fireplace working
- Set up an outdoor fireplace with large rocks to bring inside for radiant heat (this won't get you super warm but it's better than nothing)
- Have a good supply of blankets, warm clothes, and cold-rated sleeping bags

See How to Survive a Winter Storm (pg. 21) for more detailed information on staying warm. See How to Survive a Summer Power Outage (pg. 33) for more detailed information on staying cool.

SANITATION NEEDS

See Appendix 6 (pg. 185) for more information.

LIGHT

Lighting is absolutely vital, especially if there are children in the house. Nothing is more frightening than being completely in the dark during a stressful situation. Fortunately, it's one of the easiest things to plan for, as well as one of the least expensive.

Some lighting solutions are:

- Candles: stock them and learn to make them
- Kerosene lamp and fuel
- Flashlights (don't forget batteries)
- Hand crank/solar lanterns
- Matches or lighters
- Solar garden lights: store them outside to be charged during the day and bring them in and put them in vases where they're needed at night
- Oil lamps: you can recycle used cooking oil or use rendered fat to power these—they give a brighter light and can be used for reading and close-work
- Solar-powered flashlights
- Glow sticks and glow bracelets are good solutions for kids (without the risk of fire)
- We love our LED headlamps. With these, you can do things hands-free at night, like reading, knitting, or other tasks that require steady illumination
- Adjust your schedule to sleep when it's dark and do tasks like reading when it is light outside to save lighting resources

TOOLS AND SUPPLIES

Some basic items will make your life much easier during an emergency. Here are some things that are essential in the event of a power outage:

- Lighter/waterproof matches/magnesium fire starter
- Batteries in various sizes
- Manual can opener (and a backup, just in case)
- Basic tools: pliers, screwdriver, wrench, hammer
- Duct tape
- Super glue
- Sewing kit
- Bungee cords
- Survival knife
- Multi-tool

FIRST AID KIT

See Appendix 8 (pg. 197) for more information.

SPECIAL NEEDS ITEMS

These are items that will be unique to every family. Consider the things that are needed on a daily basis in your household. It might be prescription medications, diapers, or special foods. If you have pets, you'll need supplies for them, too. The best way to figure out what you need is to jot things down as you use them over the course of a week or so.

Generators are not a practical investment for long-term preparation.

The fuel-generated lifestyle will only last for as long as you have . . . well . . . fuel. Very few of us have enough storage space or the proper facilities to store five years' worth of fuel. If the power grid goes down in a catastrophic way, it's going to take at least five years to get things up and running again, and that's assuming things *ever* get up and running in the way they are now.

That means that people are spending thousands of dollars investing in items that will only sustain their lifestyles for a brief period of time. Generators are not a long-term solution unless you have renewable power. (More on that later.) While a generator would be a blessing in a short-term emergency (think a week-long power outage due to a storm), for a permanent way of life they are completely impractical.

Furthermore, in the event of an EMP strike, if your generator is not protected, it may not work no matter how much fuel you have stored.

Maybe the fact that I'm not rolling in money is the reason I feel this way. Maybe people with lots of money to spare have ideas about how to keep their generators running forever. But for my personal situation, this is a preparation strategy that is completely impractical. In my opinion, a low-tech lifestyle is the best way to prep for grid-down survival.

If money is an object in your preparedness endeavors (and let's face it, money is an object for most of us these days), then focus your dollars on preps that are sustainable without electrical power. Instead of trying to live the exact same life you are living right now, only fueled by an individual generator, look for low-tech solutions instead. This reminds me of people who stop eating gluten but still want to eat exactly like they have been eating their entire lives, only now with expensive gluten-free baked goods that cost four times the price of their wheat-filled counterparts. When things change dramatically, accept the change and adapt to it, instead of trying to maintain the illusion that everything is the same.

Renewable power is practical power.

One exception to my no-generators rule is renewable power. If you can afford a solar set up for your home, then very little would change about your day-to-day life, aside from you being one of the few people with power. You don't have to go totally solar to have power for a few important items. Assuming you have electronics in working order, they can be powered with solar, wind, or water.

Most of us can't afford an entire setup but these are some options to consider:

- Solar generators
- Portable solar recharging stations
- Solar-powered systems for specific items
- Wind power
- Water power

The peace of mind that comes from being prepared for a disaster before it happens cannot be measured. You won't have to fight the crowds or be faced with empty store shelves. You won't have to sit there, cold and miserable, in the dark. You won't be hungry or thirsty. You will be able to face the event with the serenity that readiness brings, and this will also make it less traumatic for your children when they see that you aren't afraid.

Appendix 5
EVACUATION BASICS

Bugging out. Getting out of Dodge. Evacuation. Whatever you choose to call it, thousands of Americans end up having to leave their homes due to emergencies every year. According to FEMA:[1]

> *Evacuations are more common than many people realize. Hundreds of times each year, transportation and industrial accidents release harmful substances, forcing thousands of people to leave their homes. Fires and floods cause evacuations even more frequently. Almost every year, people along the Gulf and Atlantic coasts evacuate in the face of approaching hurricanes.*

Despite this, many people seem to be taken utterly by surprise when they're told to leave their homes due to a local disaster. The ensuing panic and confusion can slow down the process for everyone, making an already terrible situation far more desperate.

The first thing you need to consider when it comes to the basics of evacuation is . . . should you? Is leaving the best option?

Should you bug out or bug in?

First, some definitions:

Bugging In: This is when you shut the gate, lock the doors, and hunker down to weather the disaster at home with your supplies.

---

1 https://www.fema.gov/pdf/areyouready/areyouready_full.pdf.

Bugging Out: This is when you grab your bug-out bag and hit the road to go somewhere else because your home is not safe.

In all but the most desperate circumstances, my personal plan is bugging in. Being out on the road in the midst of a disaster means you're a refugee. It means your supplies are minimal and that the things you've carefully stored over the years are very possibly going to be lost to you. The personal sustainability you've been cultivating at your home is also out of reach, including your garden, your livestock, and your water plan.

However, this is not a decision that's engraved in stone. Remember the three steps to surviving a crisis?

1. Accept
2. Plan
3. Act

If you are completely married to one, and only one, course of action, it limits your ability to perform the first step: accepting that whatever horrible event is out there, has actually occurred.

You must be adaptable if you want to be able to survive extraordinary circumstances. Disasters rarely go by a script, and your plan can't either.

THE VARIABLES TO CONSIDER REGARDING STAYING OR GOING

The answer to this question is hard to come by. There are so many different variables, there can never be a one-size-fits-all response. Here are the major factors you must consider.

Will you be safe if you remain at home?

Bugging in is my first choice, but there are some situations in which evacuation is a necessity. During the King Fire in 2014, we lived in Northern California and were only a few miles from the evacuation line. Had the fire leapt that line, it would have been suicidal to stay home.

If you live near an erupting volcano, same thing. Massive hurricanes also indicate that evacuation is a wiser course of action. Chemical spills, fires, biological contaminants, and extreme civil unrest can all be good cause to get-the-heck-out. You have to be willing to accept that no matter how fantastic your survival set-up is at home, there are some circumstances beyond your control that would absolutely require a bug out.

Do you have a place to go?

Bugging out to the woods to live off the land *is not a good idea* for most people, especially those who don't already spend a great deal of time in environments like that. While there are some folks that would be just fine, most of us would not. Are you going to go live in the woods with your children, your elderly mother-in-law, and your diabetic spouse?

Even though it's a stretch, it might work briefly in good weather. But what about when the snow flies? What about when your food runs out? What about the fact that every third prepper has the same idea and will be out there shooting at deer, thus rendering your ability to bag one nearly impossible? If you do get one, do you know how to preserve it with only what you carried out to the woods on your back?

That list could go on and on. The point is, do you have a reliable retreat that is stocked with supplies? Do you have a friend in the boondocks to whom you can go? Is that friend *expecting* you, and have you ponied up with some supplies before the event to ensure that you are welcome?

If you have your own retreat set up somewhere, what will you do if someone hostile gets there first? If it has really, truly hit the fan, your best bet for bugging out is a well-stocked retreat location where someone in your group resides full time.

Do you have a way to get there?

So, you have a retreat, an awesome little compound that is up the mountain, over the stream, and around the bend. That is a wonderful thing to have. But in a worst-case scenario, how will you get to it if you can't drive? How long would it take you to hike there, should the roads be clogged by fellow evacuees, or in the event of an EMP event that takes out the power, including that of most vehicles?

Is it possible to get there on foot with the family members who will be accompanying you? How far away is your secondary location? If it's going to take you more than a week to get there on foot, your chances of making it to your destination with a family in tow are slim.

Your secondary location should be less than one hundred miles from your primary location if you expect to get there in a crisis. A twenty-five-mile range is optimal because it's far enough not to be affected by localized disasters, but not so far you couldn't make it on foot in a couple of strenuous days.

Can all of your family members make the trip?

It's important to have a plan, a backup plan, and a backup to your backup. Often, in a bug-out scenario, that plan includes a difficult hike over rough terrain. Have you thought about who you'll be taking with you?

If there are children, are they old enough to walk on their own for long distances or will you be carrying them? A twenty-five-pound child piggy-backing on you will drain your energy very quickly, especially if you are going up and down steep trails. What about elderly family members? If you have a parent who is frail, has a heart condition, or has age-related dementia, bugging out on foot is simply not an option for you unless you can rig up a sturdy cart with knobby, off-road tires, and pull it.

If you have family members that can't make it under their own steam, you must plan for your on-foot-bug-out to take far longer than it would normally. That doesn't make it impossible, it just means that you *must* take these things into consideration, in advance, and make modifications to your travel arrangements.

When to go

When to go is every bit as important as *whether* to go.

If you live in the heart of a city, civil unrest is going down, and the homes around you are getting burned to the ground by rioters, you may have missed your window of opportunity for easy evacuation.

If there are only two roads out and everyone else has decided it's time to go, you may be too late to get out quickly. For example, places like New York City and San Francisco are accessible by only a couple of bridges. With the huge populations there, getting out of those cities would be nearly impossible if you wait too long to leave.

This all goes back to the three steps to survival: Accept, Plan, Act. If the situation has shown signs of going south in a hurry, you need to get a move on. If you are going to go, go early. You don't want to be stuck in traffic sitting in your car when the hurricane hits. If the local government gives an evacuation order, that means that everyone else in your area is getting that order at the same time. The roads will quickly become impassable, as traffic becomes gridlocked and unprepared people run out of fuel.

If you do decide to go . . .

Nearly everything to do with bugging out needs to be done ahead of time. When the time comes to evacuate, you want to be able to put your plans into motion quickly and flawlessly. This reduces stress tremendously.

- **Have bug-out bags prepared.** They should contain all of your important documents in case you have to grab and go along with the things you need to survive for up to seventy-two hours away from home.
- **Have a list.** Make a written checklist that you can easily access. You might include the location of items that are packed away. Decide on these things now, when you have

the time to calmly think about what items are the most important.

- **Decide ahead of time who packs what.** Break your list down so each person in the family can have specific items for which they are responsible. Sit down well before disaster strikes and make an evacuation plan with your family

- **Get organized.** All the lists in the world won't help you pack quickly if you don't know where things are. One change we made after the King Fire is that all of the items we deemed precious enough to pack and take with us are stored in one area so that we won't have to look for them when seconds count.

- **Have multiple evacuation routes planned.** Don't rely on GPS, either. Have physical maps on hand in case you need to set out on foot.

- **Have a destination.** Please don't think you are going to go deep into the woods and live off the land. It's one of those movie-of-the-week ideas that will get you killed.

- **Keep your vehicle full of fuel.** If you have to evacuate, lots of other people will be hitting the road, too. When you're stuck in traffic, you don't want to be worried about your fuel gauge dropping to the empty mark, leaving you stranded in a dangerous situation.

- **Get fit.** If you aren't in shape, bugging out on foot through the mountains isn't going to go well for you. When is the last time you hiked even five miles? Did you have a pack on? How much did it weigh? There is a large contingent of armchair preppers who have this idea, yet they don't exercise regularly and stay in shape for this eventuality.

This is a classic recipe for a heart attack, by the way. Extreme over-exertion. High-stress situation. High-sodium, easily packable food. Out-of-shape person. A few miles into the journey, particularly if it includes a steep climb, the person will experience a pounding heart, dizziness, and faintness, as the body tries to shut down to protect itself from the unaccustomed demands. If the physical stress continues, the heart won't be able to keep up with the demand to pump blood.

This can endanger not only you, but the people making the trek with you. What if you have a heart attack halfway up the mountain? What if you have an asthma attack? What if you injure your out-of-shape self? Who is going to help you? If the situation is bad enough that you're bugging out on foot, you aren't likely to be airlifted to a hospital for medical care. No matter what Plan A is, you need to have all of the above components in place long before any potential disaster occurs.

THESE ACTIONS ARE NOT LAST-MINUTE ACTIONS

- Check your bug-out bags.
- Organize your most precious belongings.
- Discuss the plan with your family so that everyone knows what to expect.
- Make these decisions now so that when (and it's always "when," not "if") disaster knocks at your door, you're prepared to respond immediately.

Next, we'll talk about what to expect from others in order to keep your family safe and on-plan. Human nature isn't as much of a variable when you can predict their behavior.

PSYCHOLOGY 101: HUMAN BEHAVIOR CHANGES DRAMATICALLY DURING AN EMERGENCY EVACUATION

During the first wildfire we encountered in California, I joined a number of local groups online so that I could get the most up-to-the-minute information, and during this time, I took lots of notes of my observations. One thing that was very clear, is that those who were at least somewhat prepared handled the situation far better than those who simply couldn't accept that this threat was real and that it was happening to them

As someone who has studied preparedness for many years, I witnessed firsthand the classic exemplar of human behavior during a disaster. As we watched the events unfold, some people changed dramatically.

During our own experience, here are the things I witnessed. They could apply to any type of disaster, natural or otherwise:

- **Unprepared people panic.** Some people panicked initially. When we got the first evacuation alert (a notice that evacuation was highly likely within the next twenty-four hours), a woman who lived down the street was wailing and sobbing as her husband tried to pack up their vehicle. She was rendered absolutely useless by fear. Meanwhile, my thirteen-year-old (at the time) was fulfilling her list while I fulfilled mine and we quickly made an orderly stack of important belongings, then turned on a movie to beat the stress. Had our area actually been forced to evacuate, those who panicked would have either been the last to leave, or they would have forgotten important things as they left in a disorganized rush. It's important to decide ahead of time who packs what, and for each person to have a list.
- **The criminals come out, like cockroaches.** Within twenty-four hours of the first evacuations, we learned that the local scumbags had looted some of the homes that had been left unattended. Within forty-eight hours, we learned that the scourge had reached the outlying areas, with these people breaking into cars that had been loaded up with the things that families had determined to be most important to them. Of course, if you've evacuated, there's nothing you can do about what's happening to your home. But before evacuation, or in the event of civil unrest, it's vital to be prepared

to defend your family and belongings. In these situations, the first responders are busy, and that's what criminals rely on. You should consider yourself to be completely on your own.

- **The longer the stress lasts, the worse some people behave.** As continued stress is applied, the true nature of a person becomes evident. People who formerly seemed like perfectly nice individuals were on the local message forums saying terrible things to one another. They were verbally attacking others for imagined slights and taking offense at things that would normally never ruffle feathers. Some folks were launching tirades against the very people who were performing the greatest service: the admins of the webpages who worked round the clock to keep us informed. If it was this bad in a *potential* emergency, can you imagine how bad things would get in a truly devastating *existing* scenario?

- **But then . . . some people are wonderful.** Alternatively, sometimes you see the very best of human nature. The generosity of many of my neighbors cannot be overstated. They housed livestock, pets, and families full of strangers during the evacuation. People showed up at the shelter with food and comfort items for those who had been evacuated. Firemen who came from near and far to fight the blaze were constantly being treated to meals at local restaurants, as other diners surreptitiously paid their tabs. Watching the kindness and gratitude helped to restore some of my faith in human nature, after seeing the squabbling and crime.

It was interesting to me that the people who gave the most generously were the ones who were the most prepared. These folks were calm and could focus on other things besides "Oh my gosh, I don't know what to do!" We definitely learned who the people were that we wanted to surround ourselves with when the S *really* HTF.

The difference between the people who crumbled, becoming easily offended, snarling, and hysterical, and the people who were generous, calm, and effective? Their levels of preparedness, both mental and physical.

WHAT TO PACK

Here are the things to pack for an evacuation. When you make your own list, remember to break these down depending on whether you have fifteen minutes, an hour, or a day or more to get ready.

- Bug-out bags
- Cell phone
- Address book with important contacts
- Money, credit cards
- Pet carriers: I prefer the hard-sided ones so that our pets are sheltered better in a crowded vehicle
- Pet food
- Two weeks of clothing
- Extra shoes
- Personal hygiene items
- Documents (identification, insurance, passports, etc.)
- A utility bill or other proof of residence
- Small portable safe for valuables
- Family photos
- Items of sentimental value
- Reading material
- Laptops
- Water
- A small fire extinguisher
- Extra fuel in a safe container
- Phone and laptop chargers
- Car charger

Your list might also include:

- Security items for children
- Items to entertain children
- Prescription medication
- Allergy medication
- Religious items for comfort
- Food (If you go to an evacuation shelter, you may end up having to purchase meals out or make due with very small rations)
- Bedding

Make a written checklist that you can easily access. You might include the location of items that are packed away. Decide on these things now, when you have the time to calmly think about what items are the most important.

IMPORTANT ITEMS THAT SOME LISTS OMIT

First of all, I can't emphasize enough the importance of those senti-mental items. Because we have lost some very dear loved ones (both my father and my children's father) we have some things that could never, ever be replaced even with the best insurance policies in the world.

- Photographs from the days well before the digital age
- Special gifts given to us by those who are now gone
- Things from their childhood (I have a music box that my father played with as a little boy, and my daughter has her father's letterman jacket)
- Journals and letters

This is a sobering thought, but if you have to leave your home because of a disaster, it's possible that you may never be coming back. Identify the things that are dear to your heart and put them in a place where you can grab those treasures quickly. Insurance can't replace these things. They can't replace that big-headed clay dinosaur with pink sparkles that your little one lovingly made for you.

We have all of these items stashed or displayed near a bin into which they can quickly be stowed in the event of an evacuation. We have backed up the photos digitally. You can't imagine how awful it would feel to lose these things, so please take steps to make them quick and easy to take with you.

If you have room, take some of your favorite things that may not be practical right now, but that you'd really miss. Do you have a favorite suit for work? A pair of shoes or a tie that make you feel fantastic and confident? Some comfy sweats that you've spent seven years breaking in until they reached the perfect level of softness? As impractical as it sounds, these are far more difficult to replace than jeans and whatever T-shirt you grab first. Favorite things can help you feel more normal when your world is turned upside down. If the worst happens, and your home in destroyed, you will find some small comfort in familiar items.

Appendix 6
EMERGENCY SANITATION BASICS

A common cause of illness, and even death, during a down-grid situation is lack of sanitation. Keeping people and things clean, along with having a way to dispose of waste, is essential to remaining healthy.

CLEANING WHEN YOU DON'T HAVE RUNNING WATER

We've discussed the importance of clean drinking water, but you won't want to use your drinking water to keep things clean or to flush the toilet. These tips will help you to reduce your water usage but still stay hygienic.

- **Break into the supply of disposable products.** Obviously in a long-term scenario, disposable products won't be what you turn to for cleaning. However, during a short-term power outage, they can be very helpful in getting your food prep areas cleaned. Before washing extra dirty dishes in soapy water, wipe them to get most of the crud off. You can use a cleaning wipe for this, since it will hold up better than paper towels.
- **Use a container of rinse water instead of pouring water over dishes.** You can go through quite a lot of water running it over soapy dishes. Use a basin of water and

rinse your dishes by dipping them into it. The bonus is, you can reuse the rinse water when you're done.

- **Use dishpans, not a plugged sink, for washing and rinsing dishes.** Dishpans have the benefit of not letting that precious water run down the drain. When you don't know how long your shortage of water is going to last, it's important to make every drop stretch as far as possible. All of this water can be safely reused for specific purposes.

- **Reuse your cleaning water.** The water that you've collected in your basins can be used yet again if you choose safely where to reuse it. For example, dishwater or cleaning water can be used for flushing the toilet. Rinse water can be used for mopping the floor, then used one more time for flushing.

- **Clean counters with disposable wipes.** If you have no water and you're pretty sure this is not going to be a situation that lasts for months, don't dirty up kitchen linens by scrubbing the counters with them. They'll just have to be washed, using up even more of your stored water supply. (And depending on what you are scrubbing off the counters, they may need to be washed right away to keep from being smelly.) Instead, use disposable cleaning wipes. First, scrape off anything stuck to the counters. If your mess is dry, use a dry paper towel to get the crumbs off, then follow up with the wet cleaning wipes. If your mess is a wet mess (like a spill) absorb as much of it as possible with paper towels. If you absorb with regular towels, hang them outside to dry so that you don't end up with smelly, souring towels in your laundry room while you're waiting for a chance to wash them. Once the major part of the mess on the counters is cleaned up, scrub with disposable wipes. If it is a food prep area, I usually then give it a quick spray with a vinegar cleaner and a wipe with a paper

towel, because I don't want chemical cleaner where I prepare the things we eat.

- **Alternatively, use a basin and rag for cleaning
  counters.** If you don't want to use disposable wipes, you
  can use a rag for cleaning the counters. Use a basin for rinsing out the rag while you clean. Before dipping it in the basin,
  squeeze out the rag over the drain to get rid of some of the
  detritus from your counter.

- **Cleaning up after you clean up.** If you haven't used disposable cleaning products, you will need to clean up after
  you clean up. Rinse all rags well in soapy water to get the
  mess off. Then, wash the rag carefully, rinsing and wringing
  it out several times. Dip it in some of your dish rinse water
  to get the soap out. Hang it to dry so that it doesn't begin to
  smell sour. If you did use disposable products and you had a
  big mess on your hands, take the garbage out so your home
  smells fresh and clean.

- **Have a bathroom basin.** You can keep a dishpan full of
  water in the bathroom for handwashing, too. Dip your hands
  into the water, then soap them up well. Scrub like you're a
  doctor getting ready for surgery, getting into the nooks and
  crannies. Then dip your hands in the basin to rinse them
  well. Be sure to get all of the soap off or your hands will be
  itchy. After using this, you can dump the water into the toilet
  tank for flushing.

WAIT . . . THIS STUFF ISN'T VERY ORGANIC!

If you're reading over this and clicking your tongue over my use of
commercial cleaning products, you're absolutely right. These store-
bought products are loaded with chemicals that I don't want to make
part of our everyday lifestyle, but emergencies often call for measures
you wouldn't take on a daily basis. If you are running your household on stored water, you're going to have to make some choices in
order to make it last through the crisis.

For this reason, we turn to harsher products than we'd normally use. Most of our homemade products are very gentle on our skin, our lungs, and the environment. I would never revert to using these things regularly, but I can make exceptions when I need to extend my water supply.

THE KEY TO CLEANING IN THE MIDST OF A WATER DISASTER

When you are cleaning up in a power outage situation, the key to success is not to end up with a bigger mess that requires even more water. I rarely use disposable products, but I do keep them on hand for those times during which we must rely on our water storage.

Here are the items I recommend keeping on hand for water emergencies:

- Disposable bleach wipes
- Super absorbent paper towels
- Basins
- Baby wipes (These can be used for hand washing and personal hygiene.)
- Your regular spray cleaner (Ours is vinegar and orange essential oil.)
- Kitty litter. (This soaks up messes and helps to absorb odor.)

USING THE BATHROOM IN AN EMERGENCY

Well before an emergency happens, you need to look at your options for sanitation. Does your toilet still flush when the electricity is out? Do you remember during the aftermath of Superstorm Sandy when residents of high-rise apartment buildings couldn't flush because the city water system was down? There were numerous reports that people were so desperate that they were defecating in the hallways. One resident of a senior apartment complex, Anna Hay,[1] said, "They can't go upstairs to go to the bathrooms. Where are they going to go? They're walking all around for a place to go. There's nowhere to go in this area."

When we lived in our cabin, the toilet wouldn't flush without power because the pump was electric. Did you ever stop to put some thought into the flushing power of your toilet? It's one of those things we in modern society take for granted. We use the restroom, then we flush, wash our hands, and forget it. But during extreme scenarios, this isn't always so easy. When researching my book, *The Prepper's Water Survival Guide*, I spent a lot of time reading about water, sanitation, and waterborne illnesses. These issues are all closely linked, and it's vital to find solutions.

If you're on a septic system, you have a safe place for your waste to go during most types of disasters, assuming you have additional water on hand for flushing. If you are on a septic system *with no risk* of the toilet backing up into the house, simply store some water for flushing in the bathroom and make use of your gray water from the kitchen. (At the first sign of a storm, we always fill the bathtub for this purpose.) Add the water to the tank, and then you can flush.

But, in the city, on a public sewer system, there exists the possibility that a situation could arise during which flushing is not an option. With some very simple and inexpensive preparations, it doesn't have to come down to that. Just having a portable toilet is not enough for good hygiene and safety. If you live in an urban area, going outside to do your business may not be an option. You have to figure out a way to take care of this, indoors, while maintaining the health of your environment.

As a former city prepper, I've been through a few situations during which our toilets were inoperable due to a local disaster. Luckily, I had the supplies on hand to create a kitty litter box for

---

1   http://gothamist.com/2012/11/03/people_are_defecating_in_the_hallwa.php.

people, so my children and I were able to stay in the safety of our home without risking illness due to poor sanitation.

HOW TO MAKE A KITTY LITTER POTTY

Here's all you need to make a litter box for people:

- Kitty litter (For this purpose, get a scented one)
- Extremely heavy garbage bags (Get the kind that contractors use and do *not* skimp on the garbage bags, whatever you do)
- Your toilet or a "luggable loo"

Hopefully, you realized you weren't going to be able to flush before using your toilet. If there is waste sitting in your toilet, you're going to need to get rid of it. Not fun, I know, but if it sits there for several days, it's going to smell terrible, even with the lid down. To get rid of it, you'll need to have a bag set up with a bit of kitty litter in it. Then, use a cheap dollar store utensil like a slotted spoon to fish out the poop. Try not to hurl, because that's just something else you'll have to dispose of. Get rid of the slotted spoon because you will NEVER want to stir beans with that one again.

Now that this is out of the way, you have two options. You can line your toilet and continue to use it following the directions below, or you can switch to the luggable loo, which is basically just a 5-gallon bucket equipped with a toilet seat and a lid. The process is the same for either one.

- **If you're using your toilet, turn the water off to the tank.** (The knob for this should be on the wall at the back of it.)
- **Line the toilet with a garbage bag.** Let me repeat: *do not go cheap on the garbage bags!* You want to use the best ones you can get your hands on. The ones for contractors are designed to carry very heavy loads. (There's a horrible pun that I'm resisting making right now.) The last thing you want is for a

bag full of human waste to break as you are carrying it out of your house. Put the bag in the bowl, then pull the top of the bag down over the edges of the toilet. Put the seat down to hold the bag into place.

- **If you're using the loo, line it with a garbage bag.** Same as above, put the bag into the bucket, then pull the top edges down the side of the bucket. Put the seat down to hold the bag into place.

From here, the steps are the same.

- **Put a handful of kitty litter into the bottom of the bag to start off.** Although I don't usually like scented products, this is an extreme scenario. Trust me, you want scent. Put the bucket of kitty litter beside the toilet and put a scoop in it (about a 1 cup scoop.)
- **Now you can use the bathroom.**
- **When someone has to go, they should do their business then toss a little bit of kitty litter on top of it.** Don't go crazy, just a cup of litter should do the trick. Remember, 1 scoop for #1 and 2 scoops for #2. Put the lid down on the toilet or loo after you use it.
- **Don't let it get too heavy before taking it outside.** For the love of all things cute and fluffy, watch the weight of your human litter. It will soak up urine and turn into heavy clumps of clay. (Anyone who has ever changed a litter box knows how heavy it can get.) Remove the bag and discard it outside before it becomes a) too heavy to handle or b) heavy enough to cause the bag to break. If you're using good quality garbage bags, "a" is more likely than "b." Most likely, you'll need to take the bag out once per day. It could be more if you have a large family or if someone is ill and making abundant use of the potty.

This is obviously not a solution for a very long-term situation, because you would have to dispose of the bags of waste. However, in a shorter-term scenario, you should be able to load the bags into a garbage can outside and deal with them when services are restored.

Be certain to wash your hands well after dealing with human waste. Although I'm not usually a fan of hand sanitizer, in these kinds of situations, I strongly suggest the use of it. Your family could become extremely ill if good hand hygiene and waste management techniques are not practiced.

Appendix 7

VEHICLE EMERGENCY KIT BASICS

Many of us spend far more of our waking hours away from home, busy with work, school, or chauffeuring our kids to their various activities. Because of this, a vehicle emergency kit is vital.

Before adding any preps to your vehicle, make sure that it is well maintained, because not having a breakdown in the first place is a better plan than surviving the breakdown. Change your oil as recommended, keep your fluids topped up, and keep your tires in good condition, replacing them when needed. Particularly when poor weather is imminent, be sure to keep your fuel level above the halfway point as well. If you happen to get stranded, being able to run your vehicle for increments of time will help keep you warm. Build a relationship with a mechanic you can trust and preempt issues before they become vehicle failures at the worst possible time.

WHAT'S IN MY VEHICLE EMERGENCY KIT?

Disaster can strike when you least expect it, so now is the time to put together a kit that can see you through a variety of situations. You can modify this list for your amount of space, your environment, the seasons, and your particular skill set. Some people who are adept at living off the land may scale this down, while other people may feel it isn't enough. I make small modifications between my cold weather kit and my warm weather kit, but the basics remain the same. While you should have the supplies available to set off on foot, in many cases, the safer course of action is to stay with your vehicle and wait for assistance.

Some people feel that having a cell phone means they can just call for help. While this is a great plan, and you should have a communications device, it should never be your only plan. What if there is no signal in your area or if cell service has been interrupted? What if you simply forgot to charge your phone? In any scenario, *calling for help should never be your only plan.* You should always be prepared to save yourself.

Not every person needs every item on this list. Pick and choose the items that are important given your family situation, your environment, and your most-likely disaster scenarios. No list can be comprehensive for every person, but this one has served us well.

- Backpacks: you can store some of your supplies in them
- Escape tool: the kind that breaks tempered glass and cuts through seatbelts (be sure this is within reach of the front seat of the car as well)
- Sleeping bag specific to your climate
- Lightweight emergency tent
- Lighter, magnesium fire starter, and/or waterproof matches
- Lighter fluid (this can help start a fire even in damp conditions)
- Candles: long-burning tea lights don't require holders and still hold their form if they melt in the summer heat
- Survival knife
- Compass
- Pocket survival handbook: I like the *SAS Survival Manual*
- Flares, mirrors, or whistles for signaling
- Space blankets: Don't go cheapo on this. The better quality could save your life
- Up-to-date road atlas
- Flashlight
- Extra batteries

- Lantern
- Crackers
- Peanut butter
- Canned stew or chili, baked beans, fruit (be sure to either stock pop-top cans or pack a can opener)
- Can opener
- Cookies
- Granola bars
- A few gallons of water
- Water filtration device like the Sawyer Mini, LifeStraw, or Berkey-to-Go
- Collapsible pet dish and pet food if your dog is a frequent traveler
- Bandages, gauze, antibiotic cream, alcohol wipes, peroxide, rubbing alcohol
- OTC medication like pain relief pills, motion sickness medication, anti-diarrheal medication
- Allergy medication and an EpiPen if needed
- Basic automotive repair tools: heavy-duty booster cables, tow straps
- Hammer, staple gun, prybar, assorted screwdrivers, pliers, hacksaw
- Rope, paracord, bungee cords
- Duct tape
- Lubricant like WD-40
- Seasonally appropriate clothing
- Sunscreen
- Extra socks
- Gloves
- Hats
- Sturdy, comfortable walking boots
- Weapons and ammo of choice

TIPS FOR PACKING GEAR IN YOUR VEHICLE

I manage to fit a substantial amount of gear in my car while still leaving plenty of room for occupants. I use larger Rubbermaid tubs organized with smaller containers inside.

- My vehicle has space beneath the back seats, where we store tightly rolled sleeping bags.

- Because of extreme temperature fluctuations throughout the year, the food should be rotated out of the vehicle every couple of months so that you always have fresh food available.

- In cold weather, your water bottles should have about two inches of the water removed to allow room for expansion when the contents freeze.

- Always have a backpack for each family member. If you are forced by circumstances to leave your vehicle on foot, you want to be able to carry as much of your gear as possible.

- Depending on the laws in your state (and your interest in complying with them) weapons and ammunition can be very useful additions to your vehicle kit. I usually have a weapon on my person so I store extra ammo in my vehicle.

- Your kit should change with the seasons. Snow pants won't do you much good in the heat of summer, but extra water and a hat to block the sun will be invaluable.

- When taking a longer trip, add more food and water to your kit than you might normally keep in it.

- Don't forget about communications: you can summon help with a cell phone or a two-way radio.

Appendix 8

FIRST AID KIT BASICS

You may not need a field trauma kit that allows you to amputate limbs or remove bullets, but you definitely want to have a few things on hand. It's important to have a basic first aid kit at all times, but particularly in the event of an emergency.

Your kit should include basic wound care items and over-the-counter medications. If you want to get more advanced, there's a list for that too.

BASIC KIT

- Alcohol
- Bandages and gauze
- Calamine lotion
- Disinfecting sprays
- Hydrocortisone cream
- Hydrogen Peroxide
- Instant cold packs
- Saline solution (for rinsing eyes)
- Thermometer
- Triple antibiotic ointment
- Tweezers

OTC MEDICATIONS

If you have a baby or toddler, you should also stock these medications in kid-friendly forms.

- Anti-diarrheal medications
- Antihistamines/EpiPen
- Anti-nausea pills
- Cold medicine
- Cough syrup
- Heartburn medication
- Oral pain relievers
- Pain relief capsules
- Seasonal allergy medication

ADVANCED KIT

- Blood pressure cuff
- Blood sugar test kit and extra strips
- Butterfly strips
- Clove oil
- Dental paste to repair lost fillings
- Dental tools
- Elastic bandages/wraps
- Hemostat
- Iodine tincture
- Israeli bandages
- Lidocaine spray
- Medical tape
- N95 and N100 masks
- QuikClot/Celox
- SAM splints
- Scalpels
- Stethoscope
- Surgical gloves
- Surgical tools
- Syringes
- Tourniquets

References to have on hand:

- First Aid Manual (The Army one is really good and can be downloaded for free[1] and printed)
- *Prepper's Natural Medicine* (dealing with all sorts of illnesses and injuries with home remedies)
- *The Survival Medicine Handbook*
- *Merck Manual*

---

1   https://archive.org/details/UsArmyFirstAidManualFm4-25.11.

Appendix 9

FOOD SAFETY BASICS

Food safety is always important but especially so after a power outage. If the food in your refrigerator or freezer has been sitting there during a lengthy blackout, you'll want to know what you can safely eat and what you should throw out. You should always have a quick-read thermometer so that you can be certain your food is the temperature you think it is. Keep in mind that if you lose a great deal of food, it may be worthwhile to make an insurance claim.

This chart is from FoodSafety.gov:[1]

Food Categories	Specific Foods	Held above 40°F for over 2 hours
MEAT, POULTRY, SEAFOOD	Raw or leftover cooked meat, poultry, fish, or seafood; soy meat substitutes	Discard
	Thawing meat or poultry	Discard
	Salads: Meat, tuna, shrimp, chicken, or egg salad	Discard
	Gravy, stuffing, broth	Discard
	Lunchmeats, hot dogs, bacon, sausage, dried beef	Discard
	Pizza—any topping	Discard
	Canned hams labeled "Keep Refrigerated"	Discard
	Canned meats and fish, opened	Discard
	Casseroles, soups, stews	Discard

---

1   http://www.foodsafety.gov/keep/charts/refridg_food.html.

Food Categories	Specific Foods	Held above 40°F for over 2 hours
CHEESE	Soft Cheeses: blue/bleu, Roquefort, Brie, Camembert, cottage, cream, Edam, Monterey Jack, ricotta, mozzarella, Muenster, Neufchatel, queso blanco, queso fresco	Discard
	Hard Cheeses: Cheddar, Colby, Swiss, Parmesan, provolone, Romano	Safe
	Processed Cheeses	Safe
	Shredded Cheeses	Discard
	Low-Fat Cheeses	Discard
	Grated Parmesan, Romano, or combination (in can or jar)	Safe
DAIRY	Milk, cream, sour cream, buttermilk, evaporated milk, yogurt, eggnog, soy milk	Discard
	Butter, margarine	Safe
	Baby formula, opened	Discard
EGGS	Fresh eggs, hard-cooked in shell, egg dishes, egg products	Discard
	Custards and puddings, quiche	Discard
FRUITS	Fresh fruits, cut	Discard
	Fruit juices, opened	Safe
	Canned fruits, opened	Safe
	Fresh fruits, coconut, raisins, dried fruits, candied fruits, dates	Safe
SAUCES, SPREADS, JAMS	Opened mayonnaise, tartar sauce, horseradish	Discard if above 50°F for over 8 hours
	Peanut butter	Safe
	Jelly, relish, taco sauce, mustard, ketchup, olives, pickles	Safe
	Worcestershire, soy, barbecue, hoisin sauces	Safe
	Fish sauces, oyster sauce	Discard
	Opened vinegar-based dressings	Safe
	Spaghetti sauce, opened jar	Discard

Food Categories	Specific Foods	Held above 40°F for over 2 hours
BREAD, CAKES, COOKIES, PASTA, GRAINS	Bread, rolls, cakes, muffins, quick breads, tortillas	Safe
	Refrigerator biscuits, rolls, cookie dough	Discard
	Cooked pasta, rice, potatoes	Discard
	Pasta salads with mayonnaise or vinaigrette	Discard
	Fresh pasta	Discard
	Cheesecake	Discard
	Breakfast foods—waffles, pancakes, bagels	Safe
PIES, PASTRY	Pastries, cream filled	Discard
	Pies—custard, cheese filled, or chiffon; quiche	Discard
	Pies, fruit	Safe
VEGETABLES	Fresh mushrooms, herbs, spices	Safe
	Greens, pre-cut, pre-washed, packaged	Discard
	Vegetables, raw	Safe
	Vegetables, cooked; tofu	Discard
	Vegetable juice, opened	Discard
	Baked potatoes	Discard
	Commercial garlic in oil	Discard
	Potato salad	Discard
	Casseroles, soups, stews	Discard

Appendix 10
ENTERTAINMENT BASICS

In our electronics-addicted world, one of the most difficult adjustments for some people during a power outage is the loss of their electronic device. Not only is it a painful break from their technology, it's happening during what may be a very stressful time. And even if you aren't addicted to social media, you're still going to want something to do.

HAVE A WAY TO CHARGE DEVICES
You can get and keep charged an external battery from which devices can be charged, but a solar charger for your cellphone or other small device will be worth its weight in gold during an extended outage. You can use this for Kindles, cell phones, iPods, MP3 players, and tablets.

NON-ELECTRONIC ENTERTAINMENT IS ALSO IMPORTANT
You'll want to have a few things on hand for entertainment that doesn't require an Internet connection or a gadget.

- Get some books and save them for just such an emergency.
- Pick up some magazines and put them away so they'll be fresh and new.
- Pick up some games, puzzles, and other old-fashioned forms of entertainment.
- Do crafts like knitting, carving, painting, or scrapbooking.

FOR THE LOVE OF ALL THINGS CUTE AND FLUFFY, HAVE SOMETHING FOR THE KIDS TO DO

Nothing grates on a parent's nerves more than a refrain of, "I'm boooooredddd." Many kids are accustomed to almost-constant electronic entertainment, so the loss of that can be quite stressful.

Keep a box of off-grid entertainment supplies in an easy-to-access place. Make one up for the different members of the family and most importantly, make these items things that the kids *are not allowed to play with at any other time* so that they are novel and interesting when the time comes to use them. Include things like stationary supplies, notebooks, pens and pencils, sharpeners, crayons or coloring pencils, markers, glue sticks, glitter, puzzles, activity books, games, stickers . . . make it a treasure trove! Be sure you keep all of the supplies needed for each activity together, because it's hard to find things when your home is only lit by candlelight.

Stock up on what you need (if anything) for these fun activities before the next grid-down scenario:

- Shadow puppets
- Books
- Hide and Seek
- Storybooks: kids are especially engaged with chain stories
- Reading aloud
- Flashlight hide and seek
- Flashlight tag
- Guess the shadow
- Toys that do not need batteries, like dollhouses and kitchens, dinky cars
- Make your house an obstacle course so that the kids run around, roll over beds, etc., to get some energy out
- Card games
- Coloring
- Board games
- Arts and crafts

- Send them outside, weather- and situation-permitting
- In the summer, if the water is running, turn on sprinklers or fill a kiddie pool to help them stay cool
- In the winter, let them have snowball fights and make snowmen
- Imagination games like playing house, cops and robbers, don't step in the lava, camping in the wilderness
- Put on a play
- Play dress-up
- Collect song books (or print lyrics off the Internet) and have a sing-along in front of the fire
- Play music together (piano, makeshift drums, harmonica, spoons, castanets, etc.)
- Make puppets and put on a puppet show
- Get out those old photos and finally assemble them in scrapbooks
- Play word games like Hangman
- Play old games like jacks, pick-up sticks, and tumbling towers
- Play with building toys like blocks, Lincoln Logs, or Lego

Believe it or not, sometimes power outages can be fun.

ABOUT DAISY LUTHER

Daisy is a coffee-swigging, gun-toting blogger who writes about current events, preparedness, frugality, and the pursuit of liberty on her website, TheOrganicPrepper.com.

She is the publisher of *The Cheapskate's Guide to the Galaxy*, a monthly frugality newsletter, and she curates all the most important news links for people who want to be prepared on her aggregate site, PreppersDailyNews.com.

She is the bestselling author of four books:

- *The Pantry Primer: A Prepper's Guide to Whole Food on a Half-Price Budget*
- *The Prepper's Water Survival Guide: Harvest, Treat, and Store Your Most Vital Resource*
- *The Prepper's Canning Guide: Affordably Stockpile a Lifesaving Supply of Nutritious, Delicious, Shelf-Stable Food*
- *Have Yourself a Thrifty Little Christmas and a Debt-Free New Year*

Daisy currently lives in the mountains of Virginia with her two daughters and an ever-growing menagerie. For now. Nomads tend to seek new adventures.

You can find her on Facebook at The Organic Prepper and Prep Club, on Twitter @DaisyLuther, and on Pinterest at The Organic Prepper.

ACKNOWLEDGMENTS

Thanks go as always to my ever-so-tolerant daughters, who have dealt patiently and fondly with my eccentricities over the years. I'd also like to thank my mom and Joe for their love and support.

To my good friends and blogging compadres, thank you for the hard work, the dedication, and the friendship. In particular, my thanks go out to Cat, Dagny, Jose, Mac, Meadow, and Selco.

To my readers . . . well, you guys deserve a special thank you. Without you, I would not be doing what I'm doing. You are a constant inspiration and source of writing topics. Your kind words keep me going and your readership is very much appreciated. Without you, there'd be no blog and there'd be no books.

INDEX